THIS BOOK BELONGS TO:

_____

COPYRIGHT 2020 Hyperamazing Publishing LLC

ALL RIGHTS RESERVED, NO PART OF THIS PUBLICATION MAY BE REPRODUCED OR TRANSMITTED IN ANY FORM OR BY ANY MEANS, INCLUDING PHOTOCOPYING, RECORDING OR OTHER ELECTRONIC OR MECHANICAL METHODS, WITHOUT THE PRIOR WRITTEN PERMISSION OF THE PUBLISHER, EXCEPT IN THE CASE OF BRIEF QUOTATIONS EMBODIED IN CRITICAL REVIEWS AND CERTAIN OTHER NONCOMMERCIAL USES PERMITTED BY COPYRIGHT LAW.

This book has been designed using resources from Freepik.com & Vecteezy.com

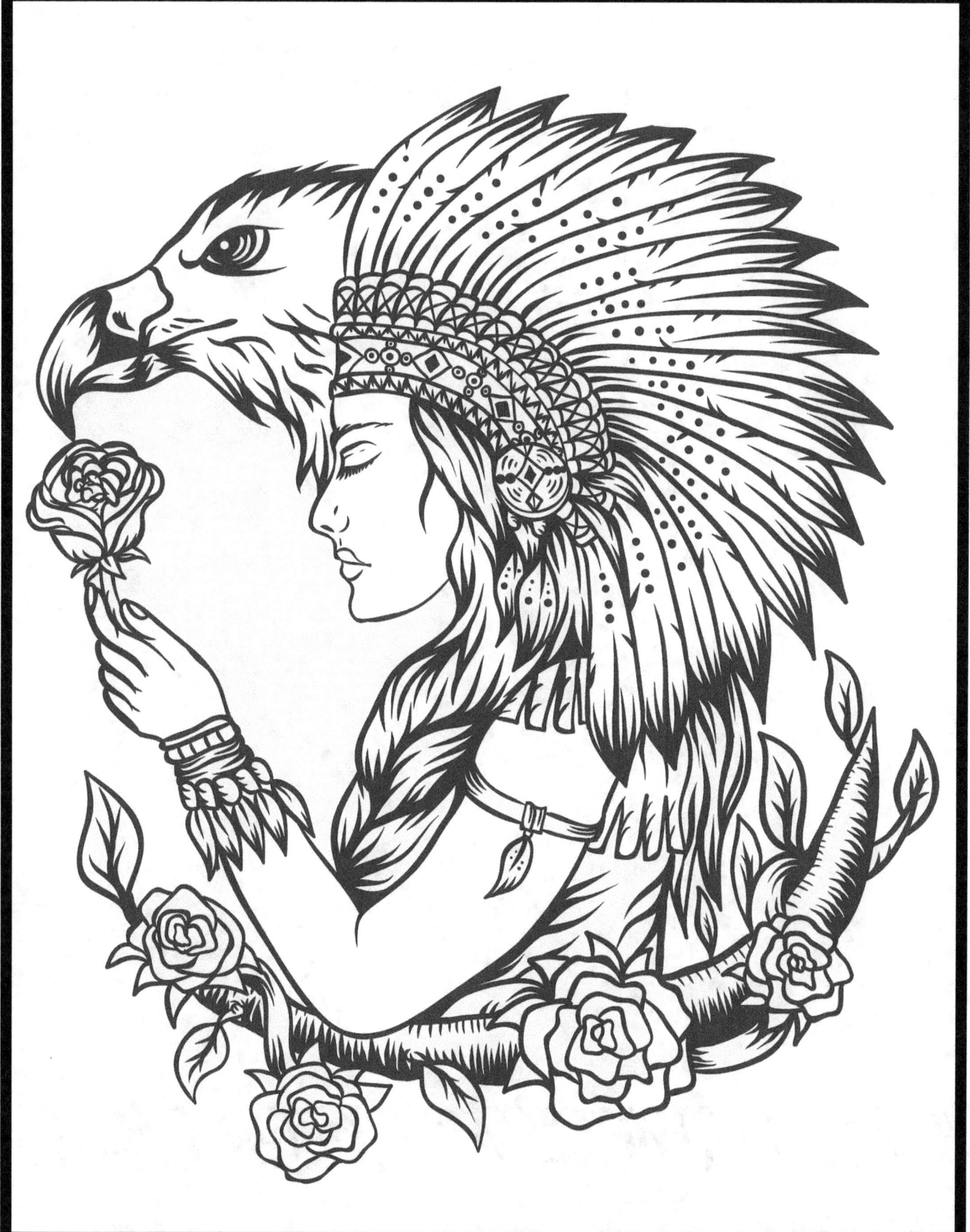

NATIVE AMERICAN GIRL & EAGLE

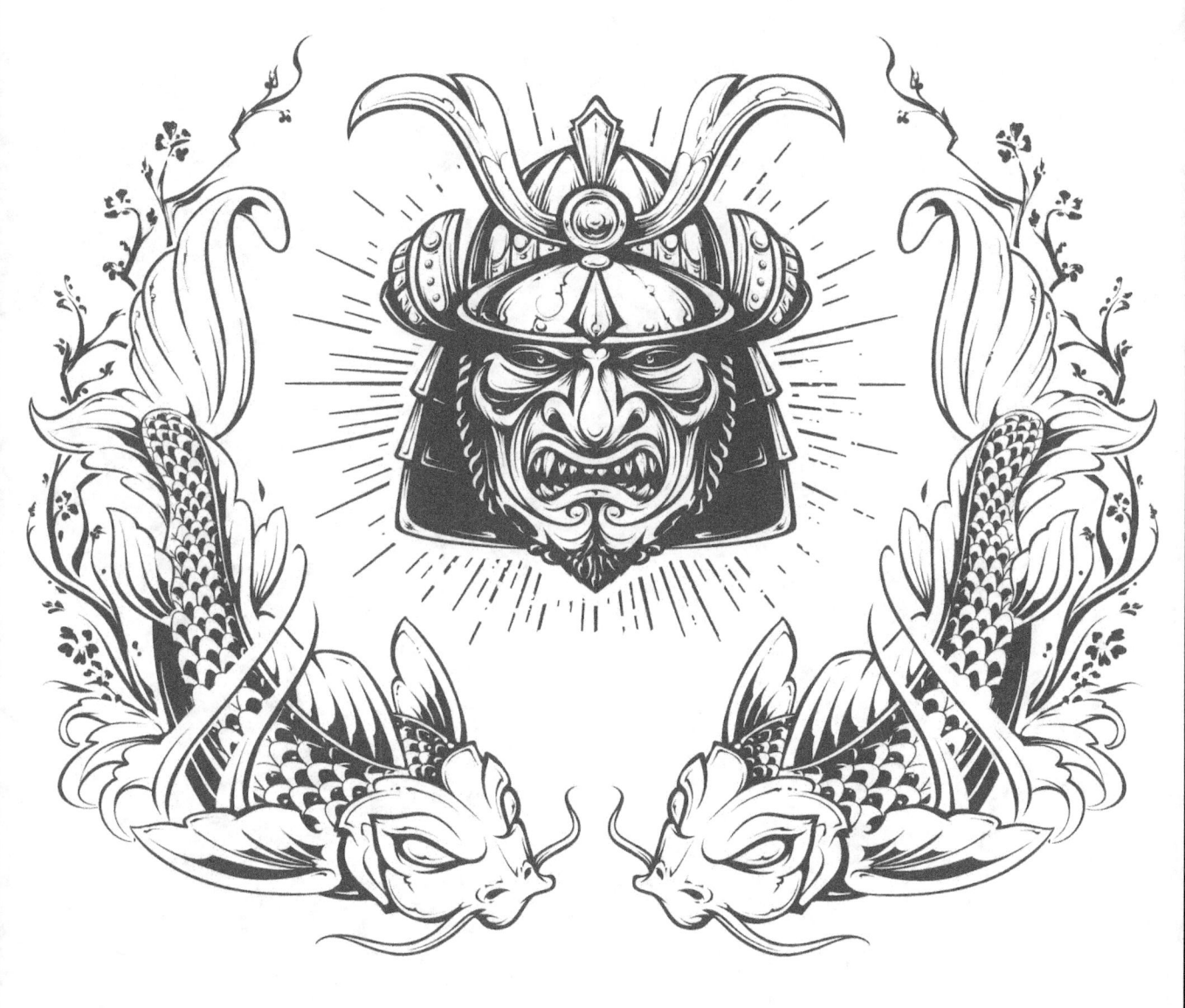

KOI FISH & SAMURAI

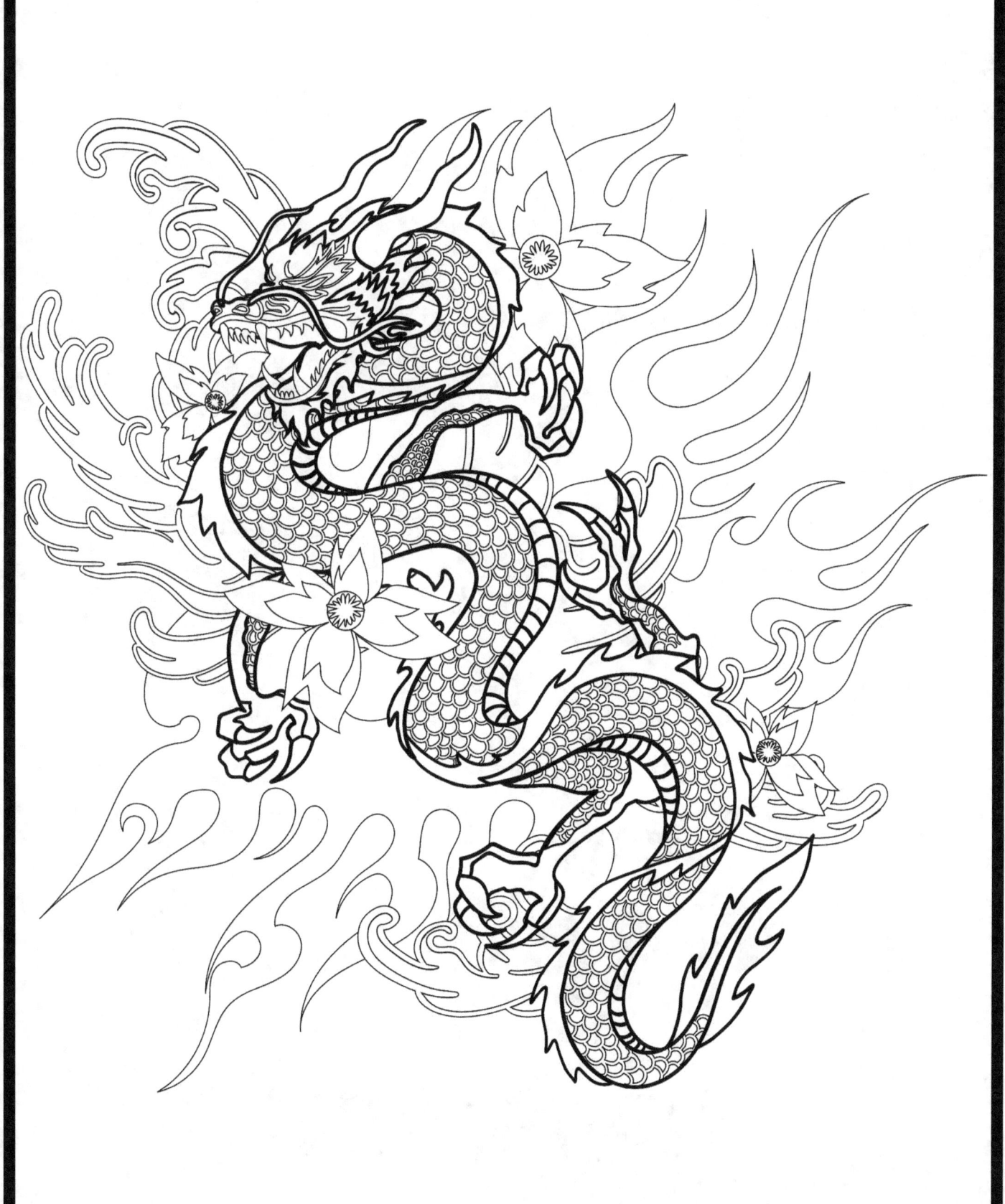

DRAGON & FIRE

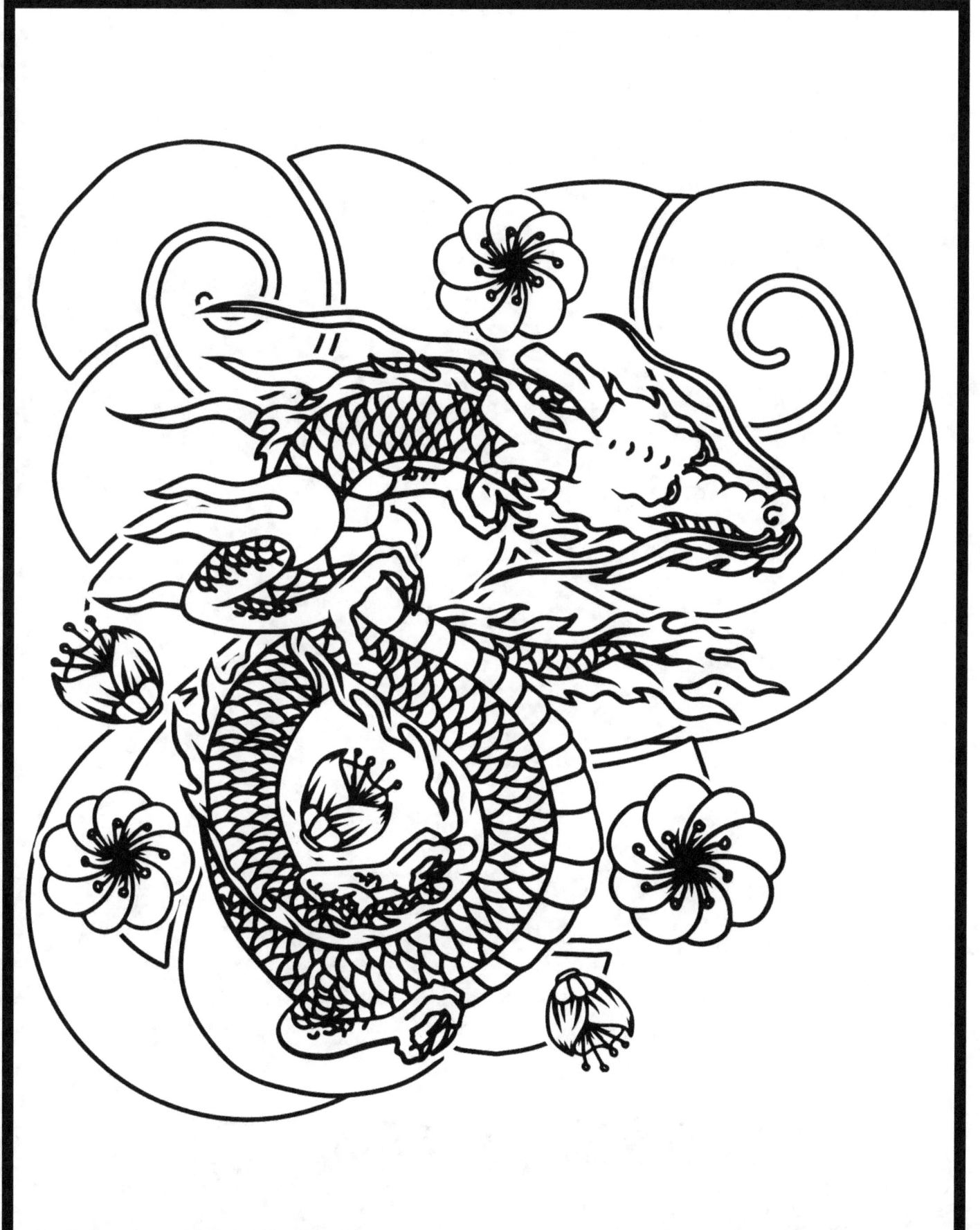

DRAGON & FLOWERS

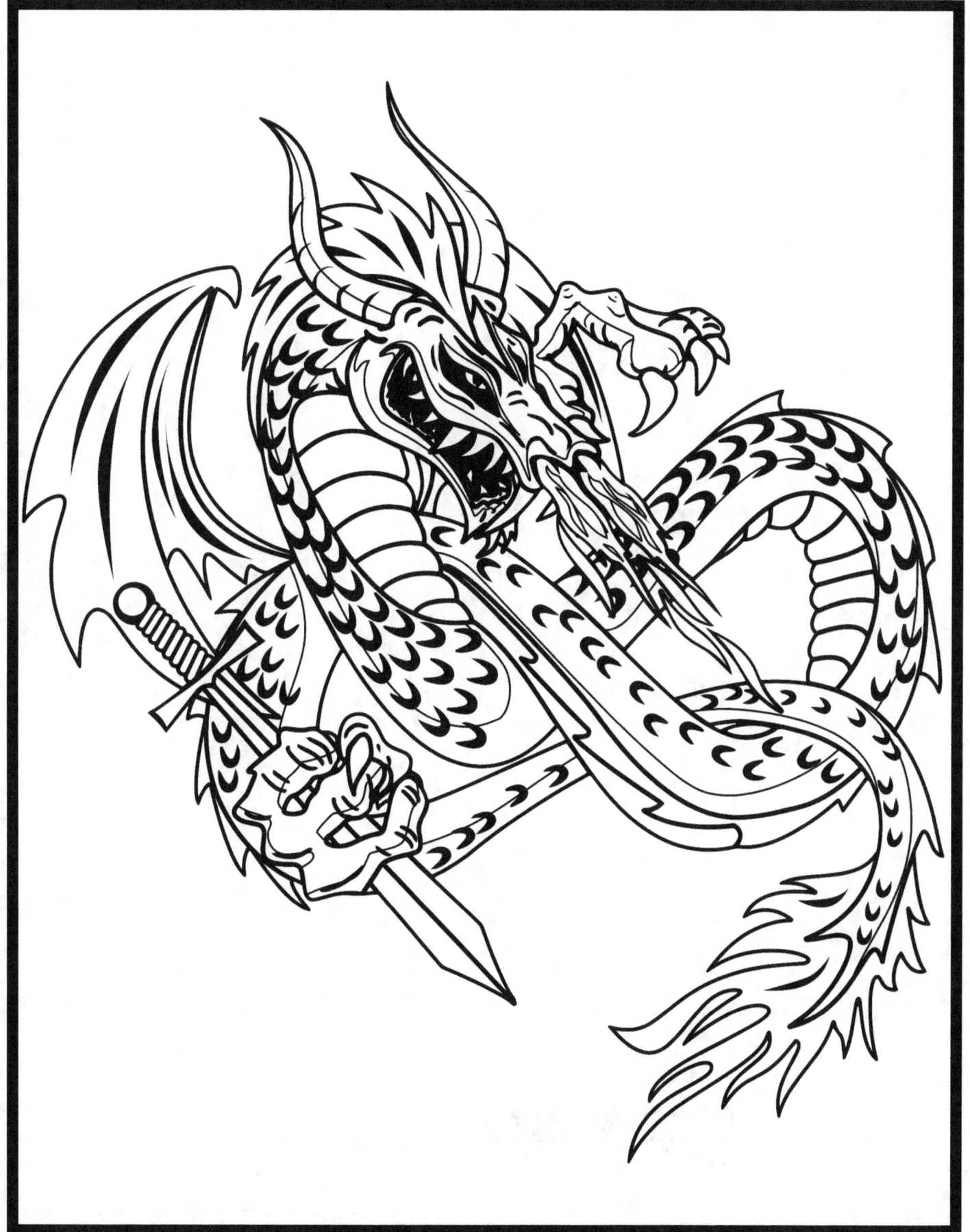

DRAGON & SWORD

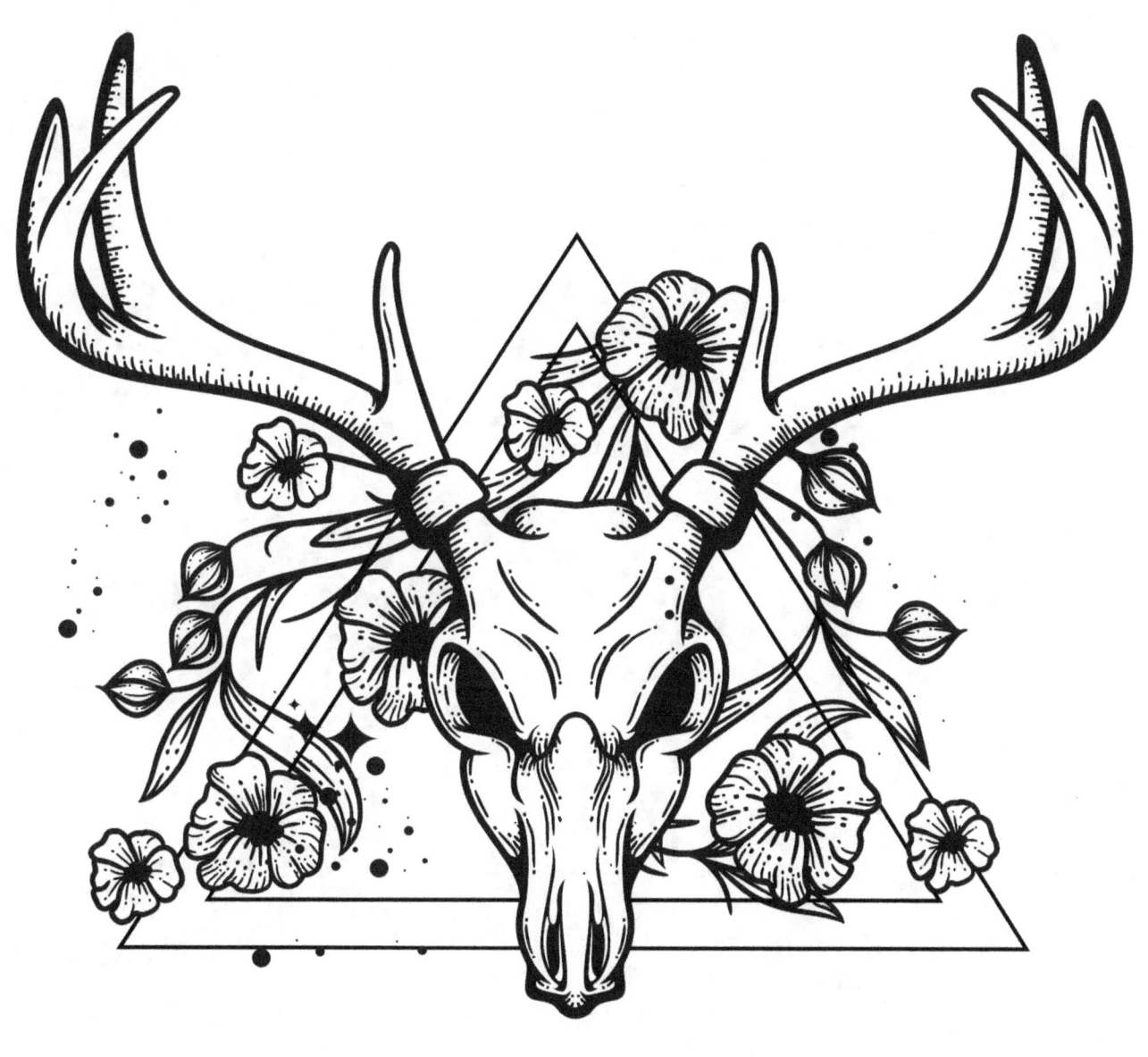

DEER SKULL

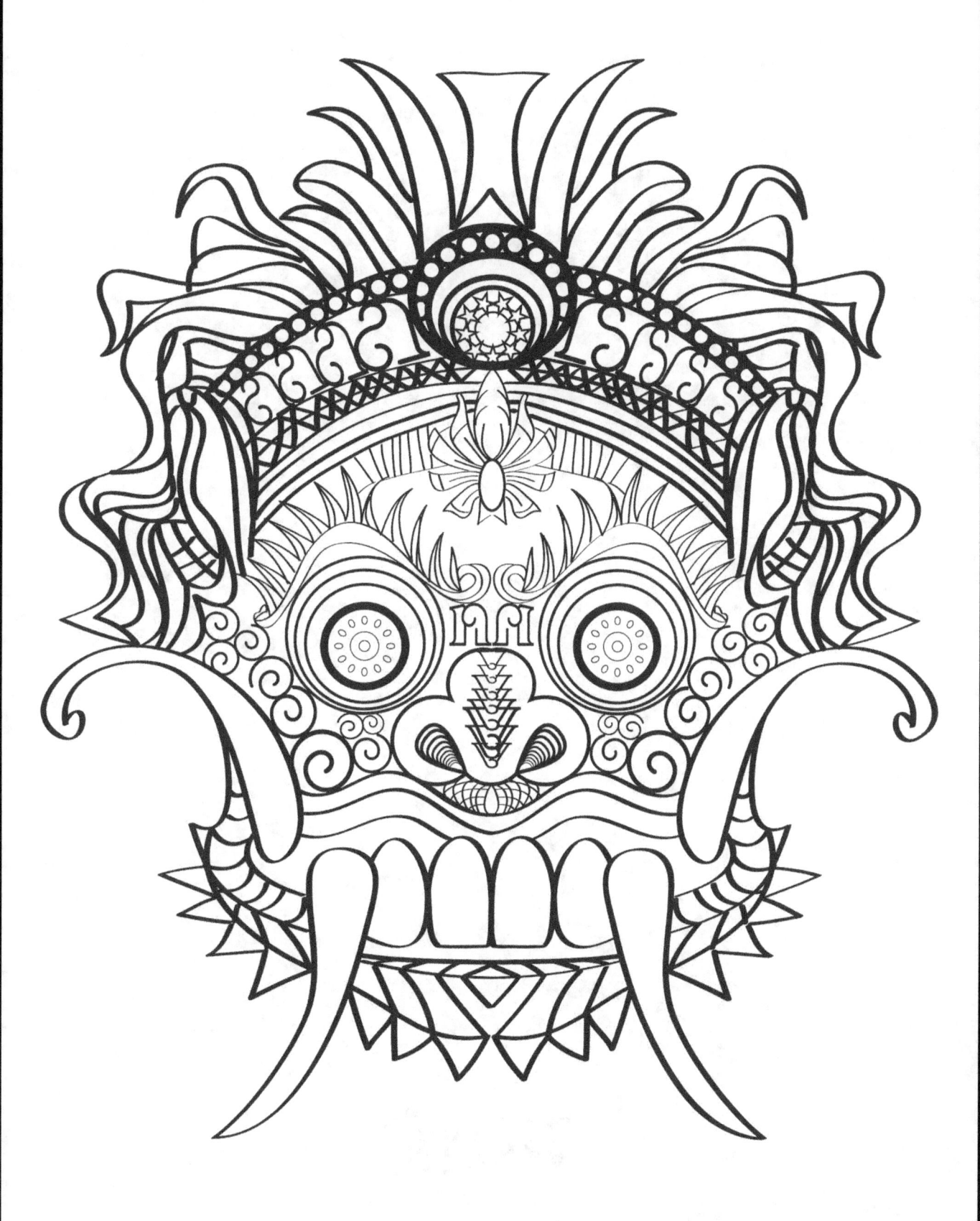

MASK

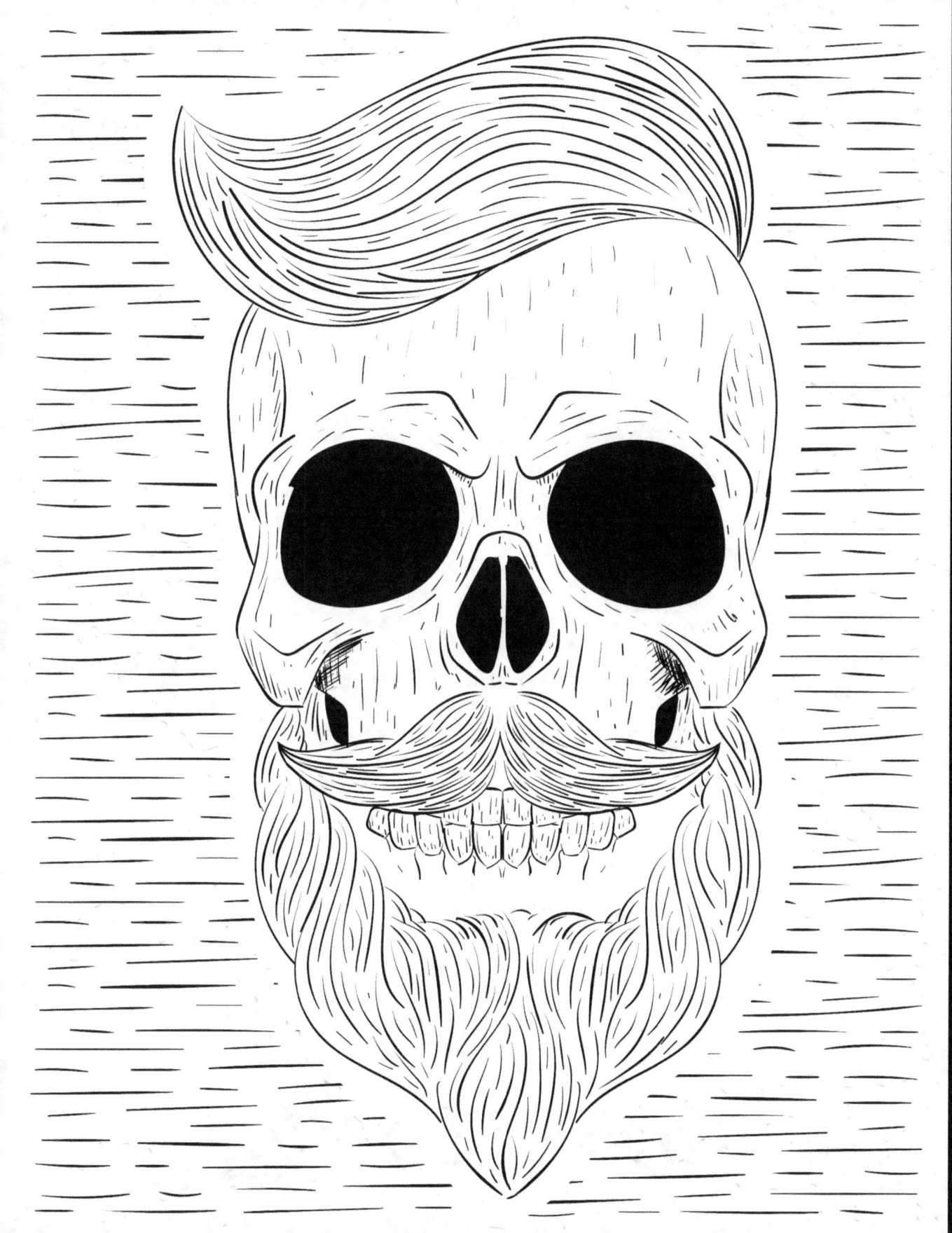

BEARDED SKULL

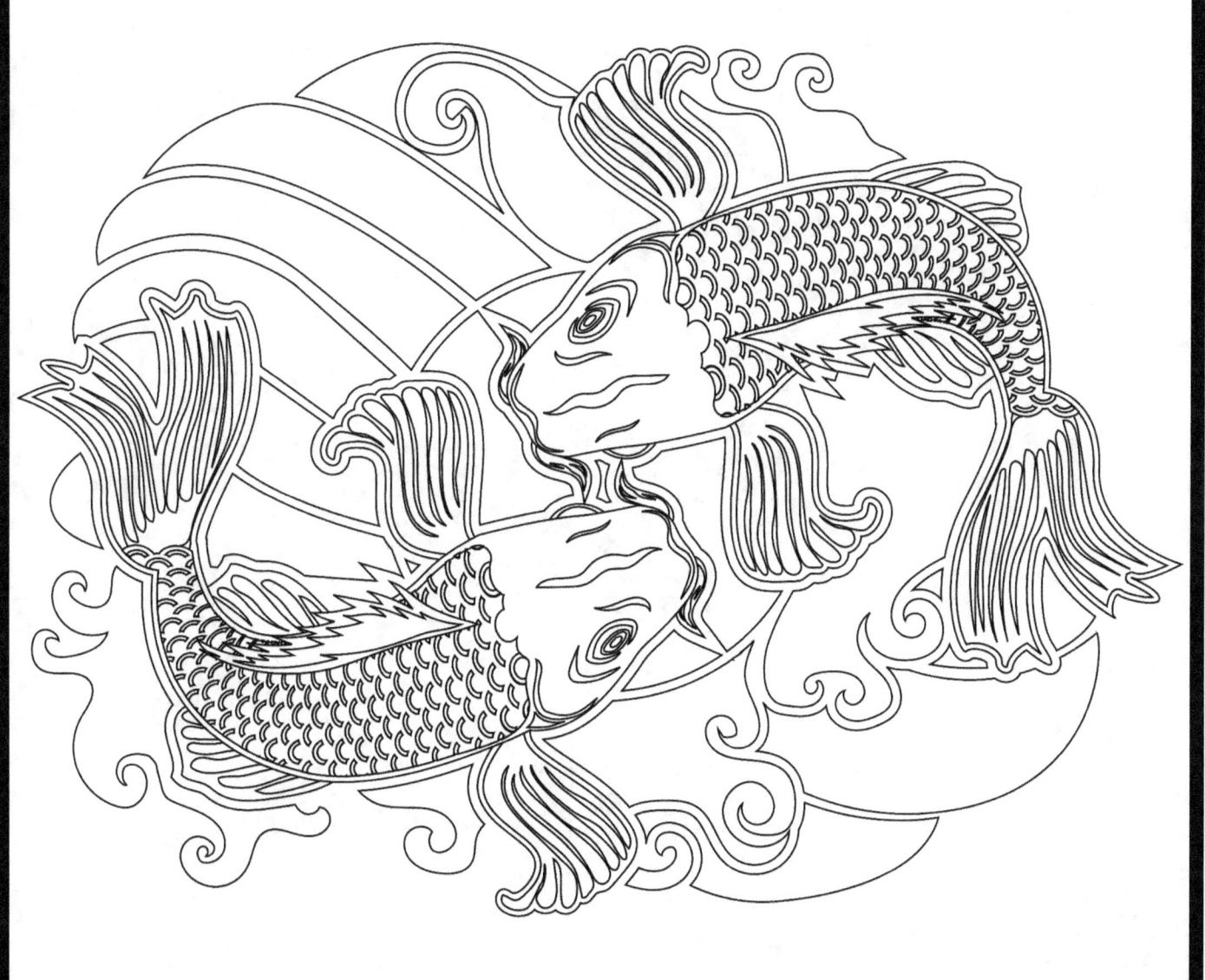

KOI FISH 1

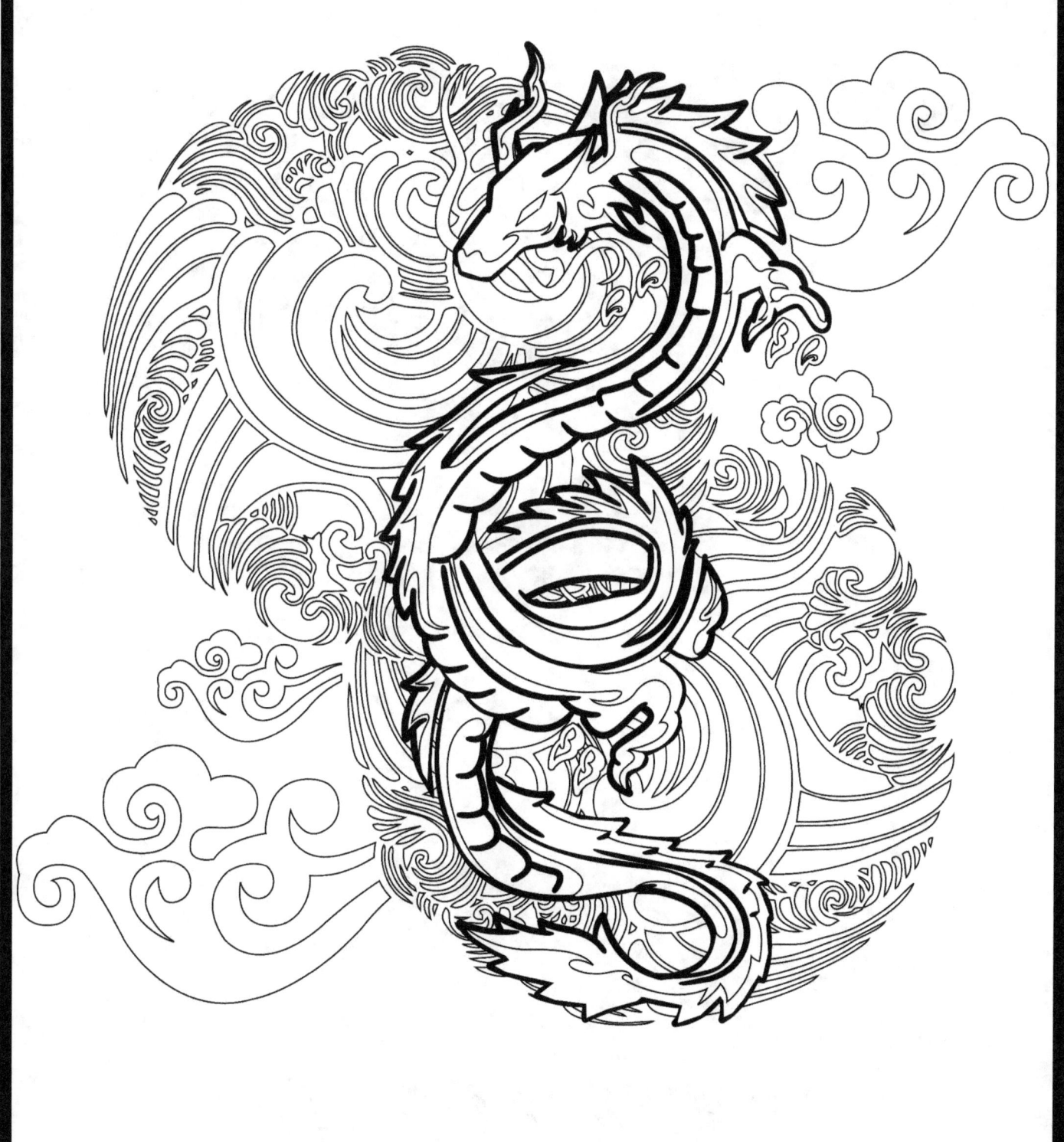

DRAGON & CLOUDS

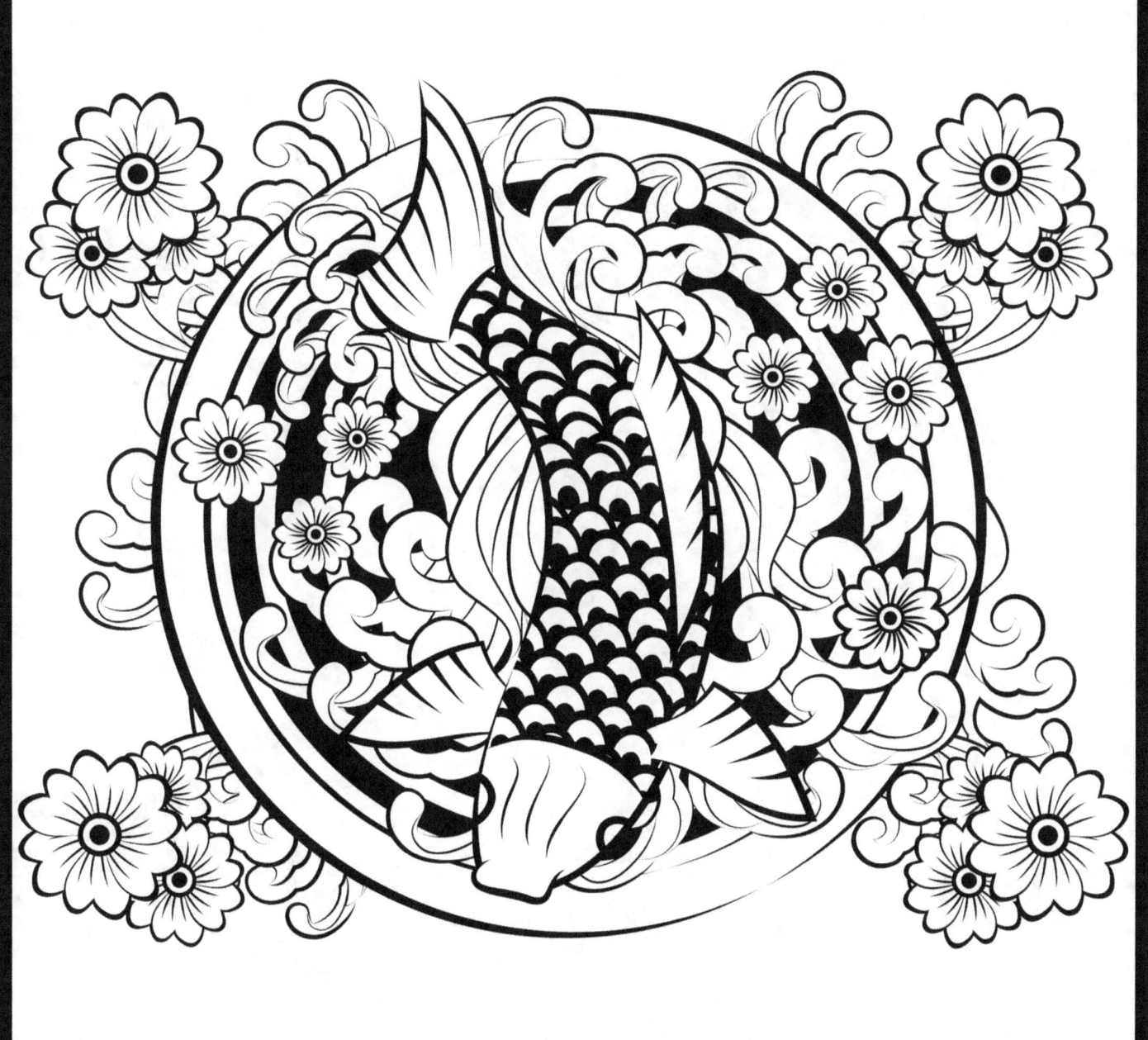

KOI FISH & FLOWERS

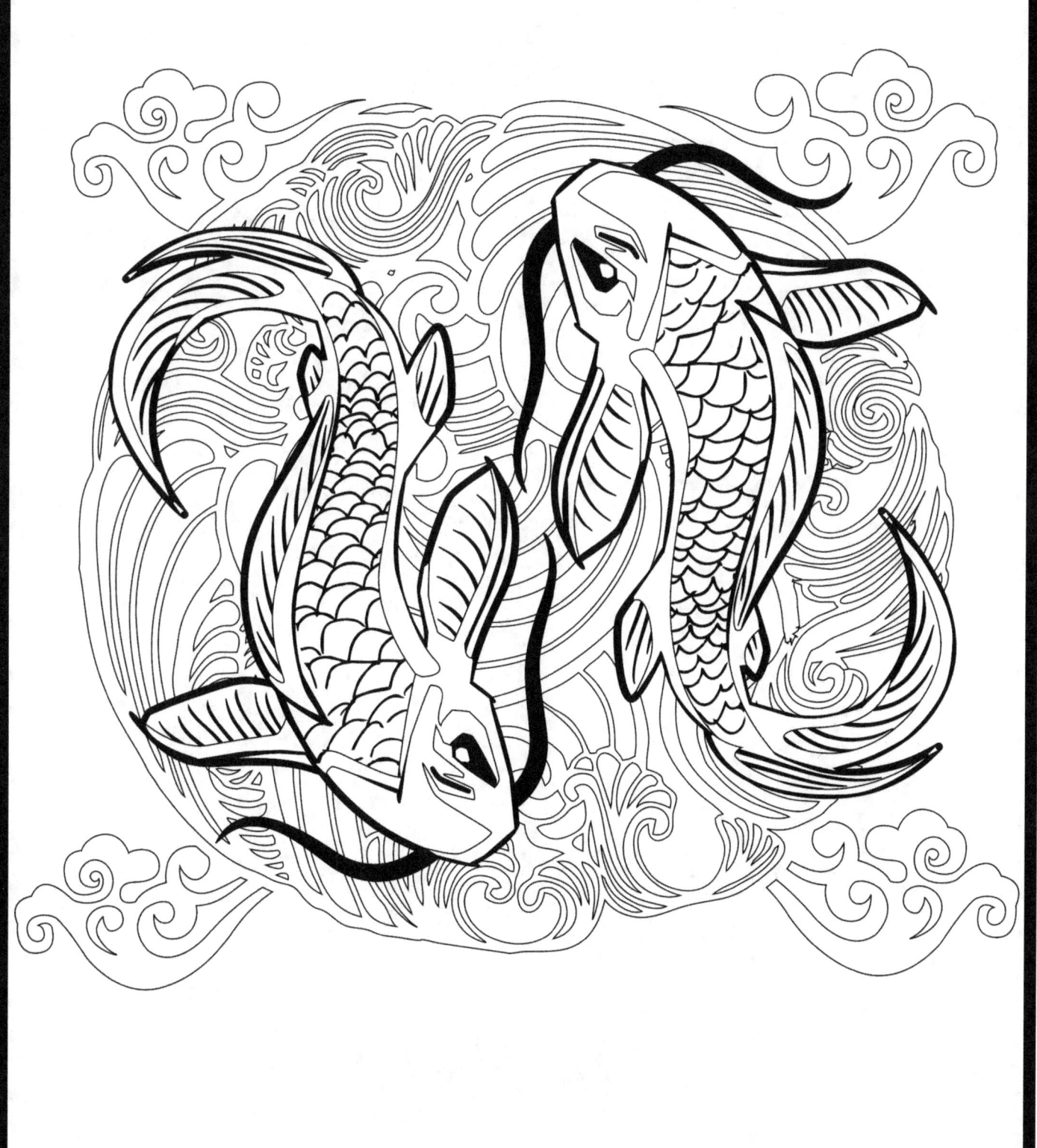

KOI FISH 2

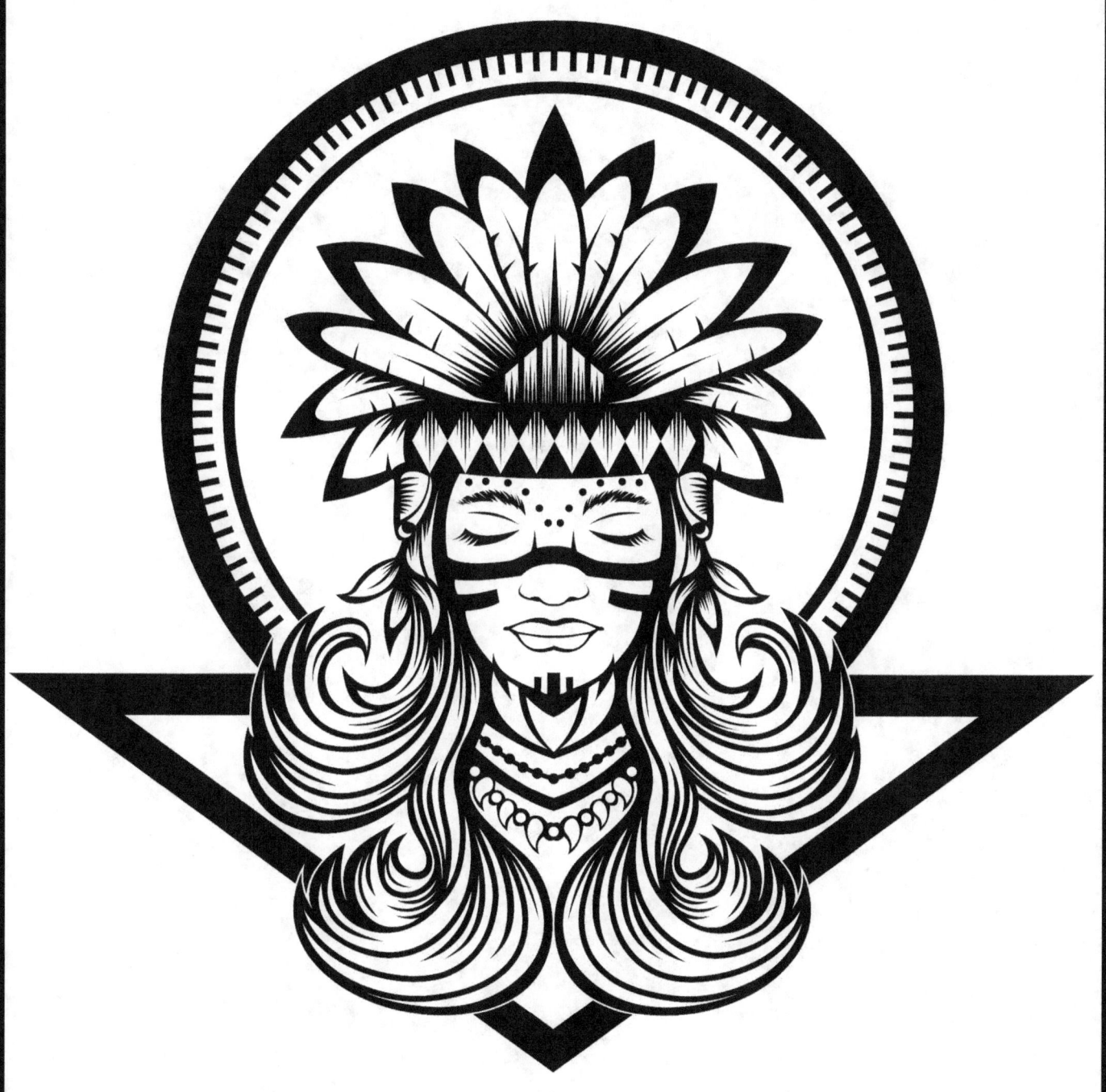

NATIVE AMERICAN GIRL

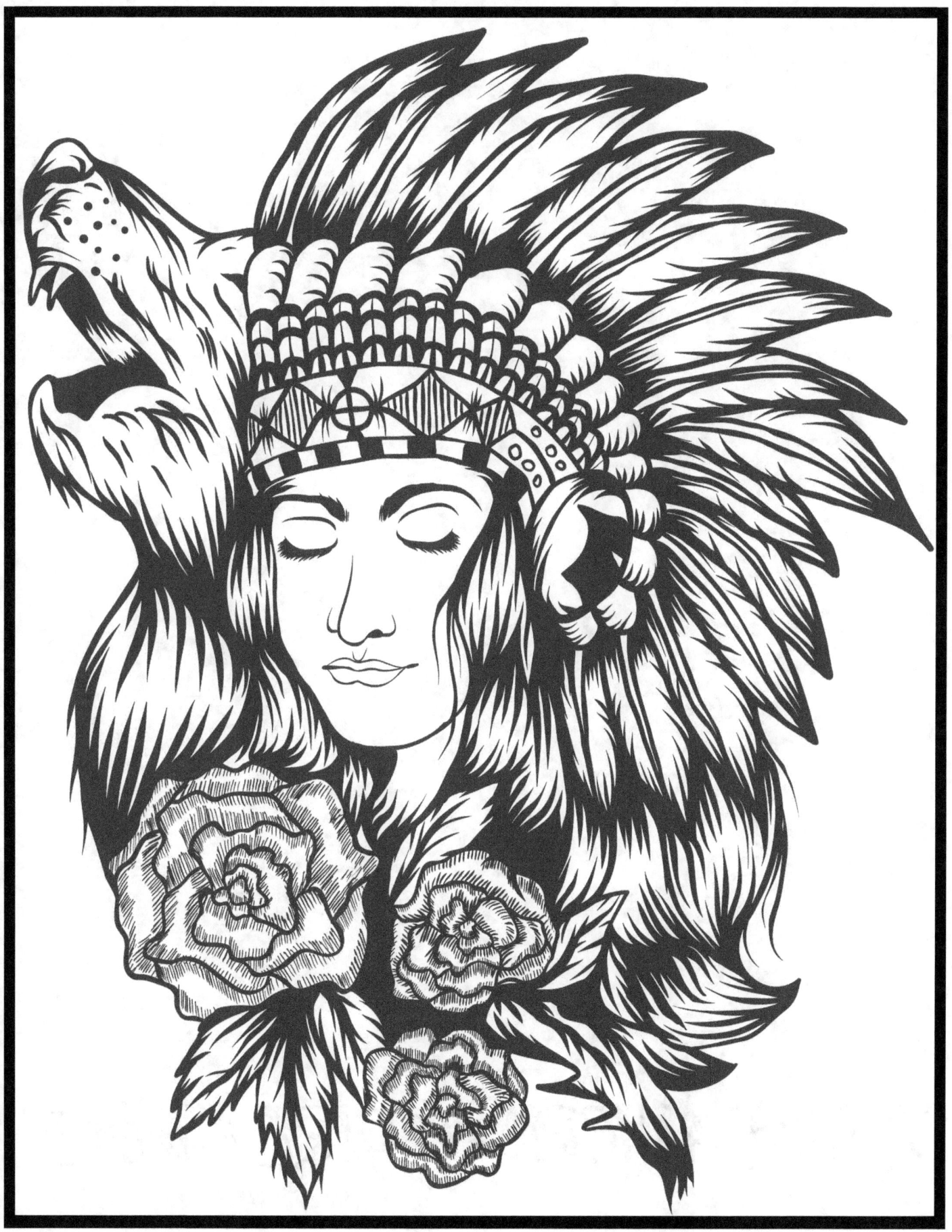

NATIVE AMERICAN GIRL & WOLF

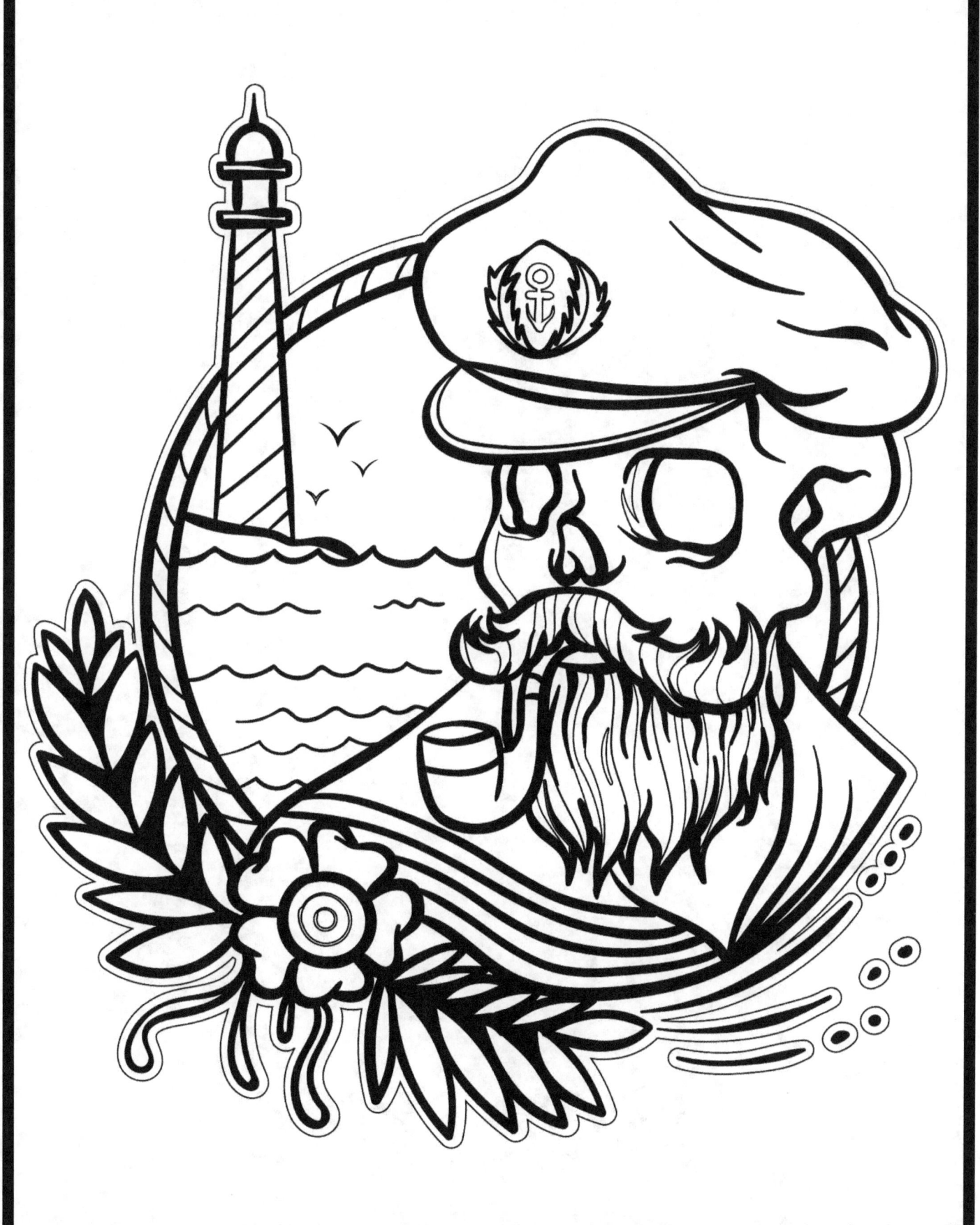

SAILOR SKULL

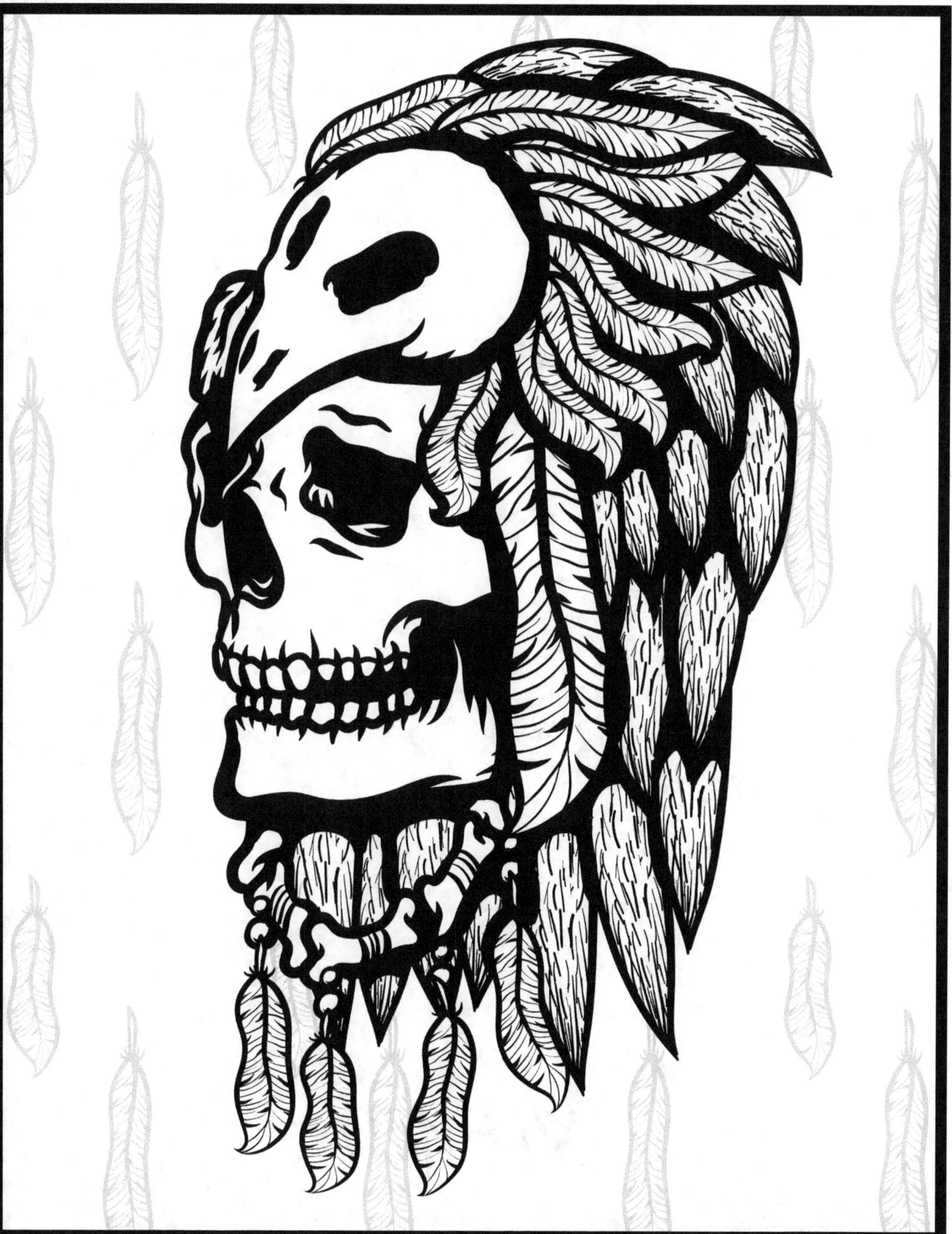

SHAMAN

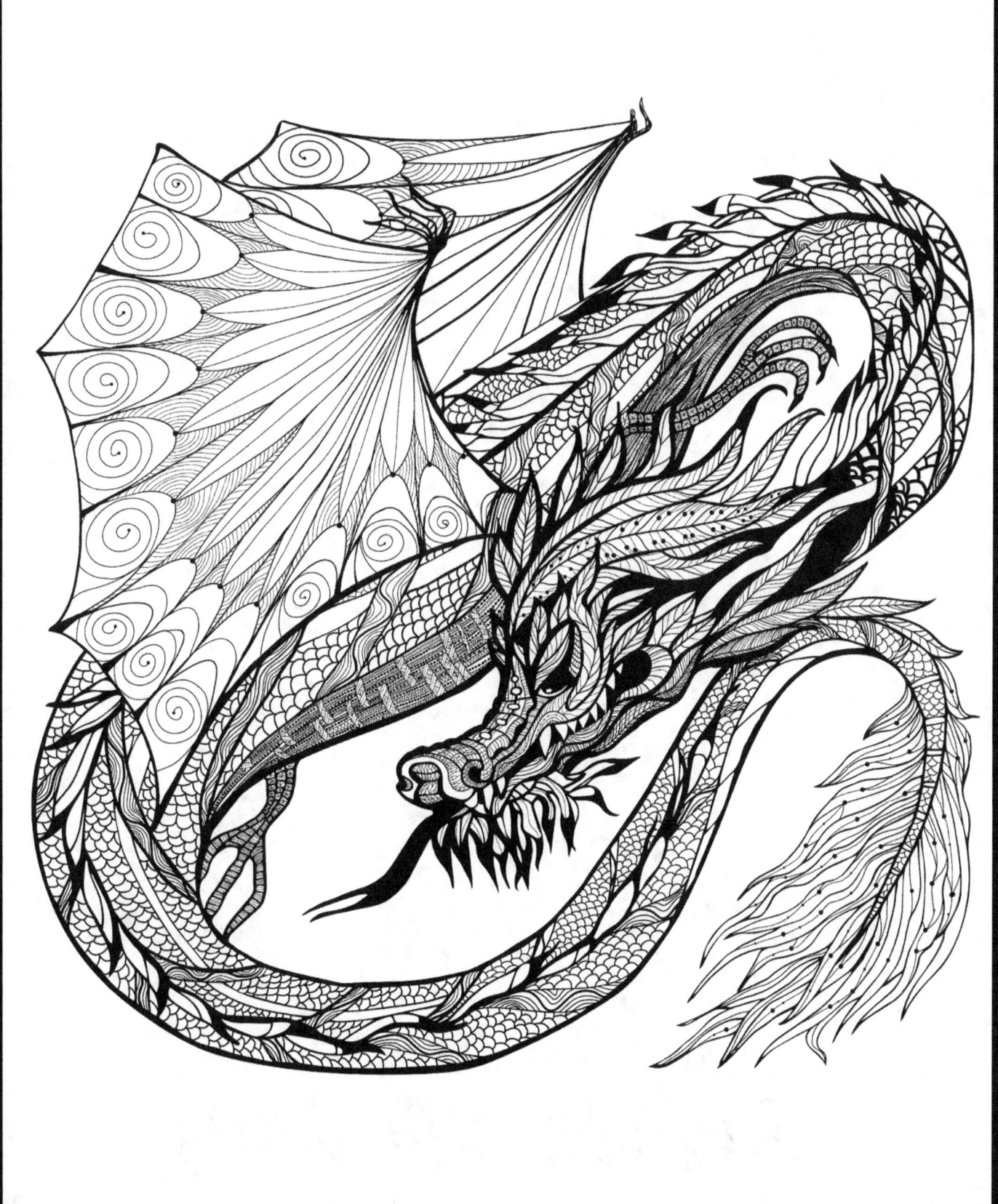

DRAGON WITH WINGS

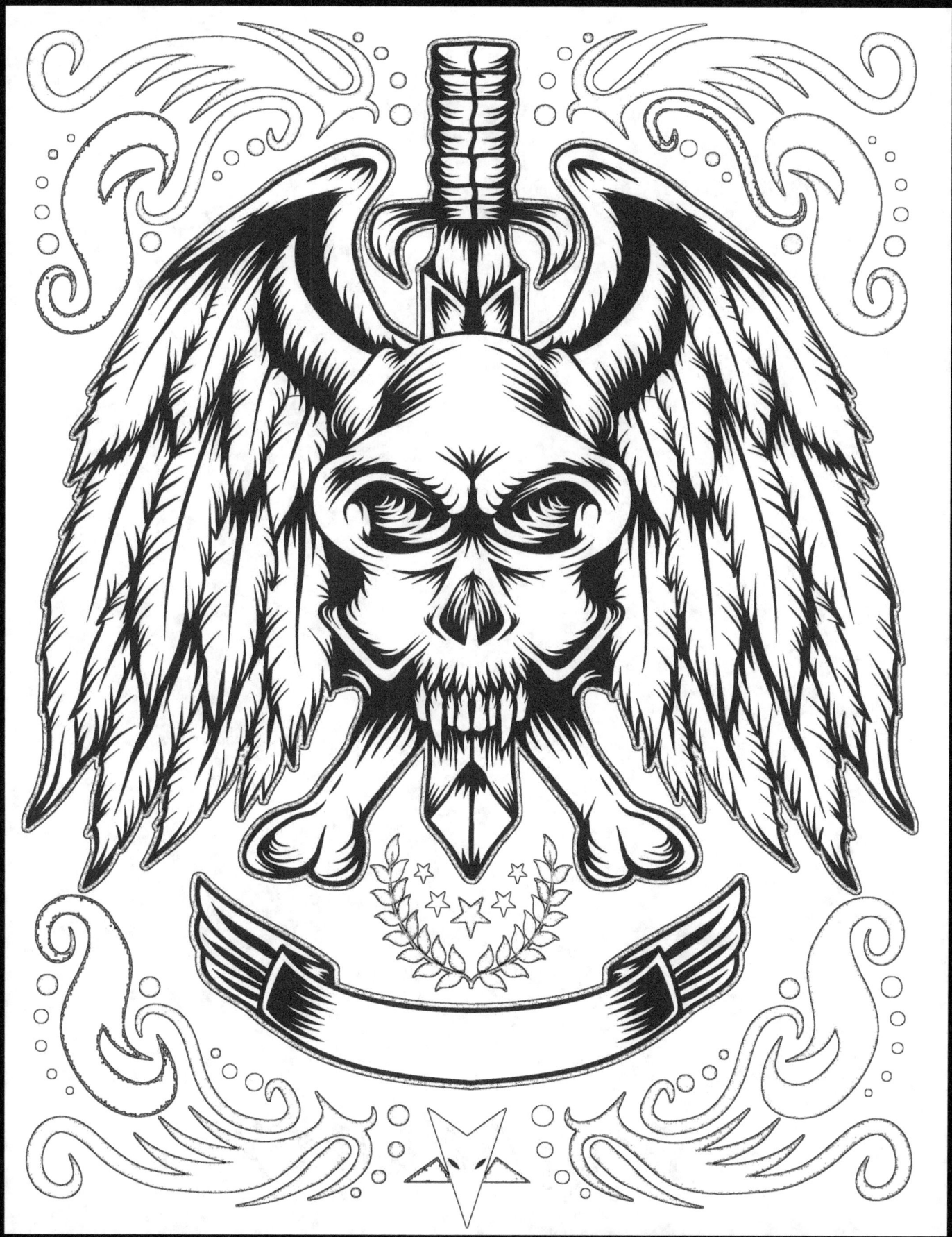

SKULL & WINGS

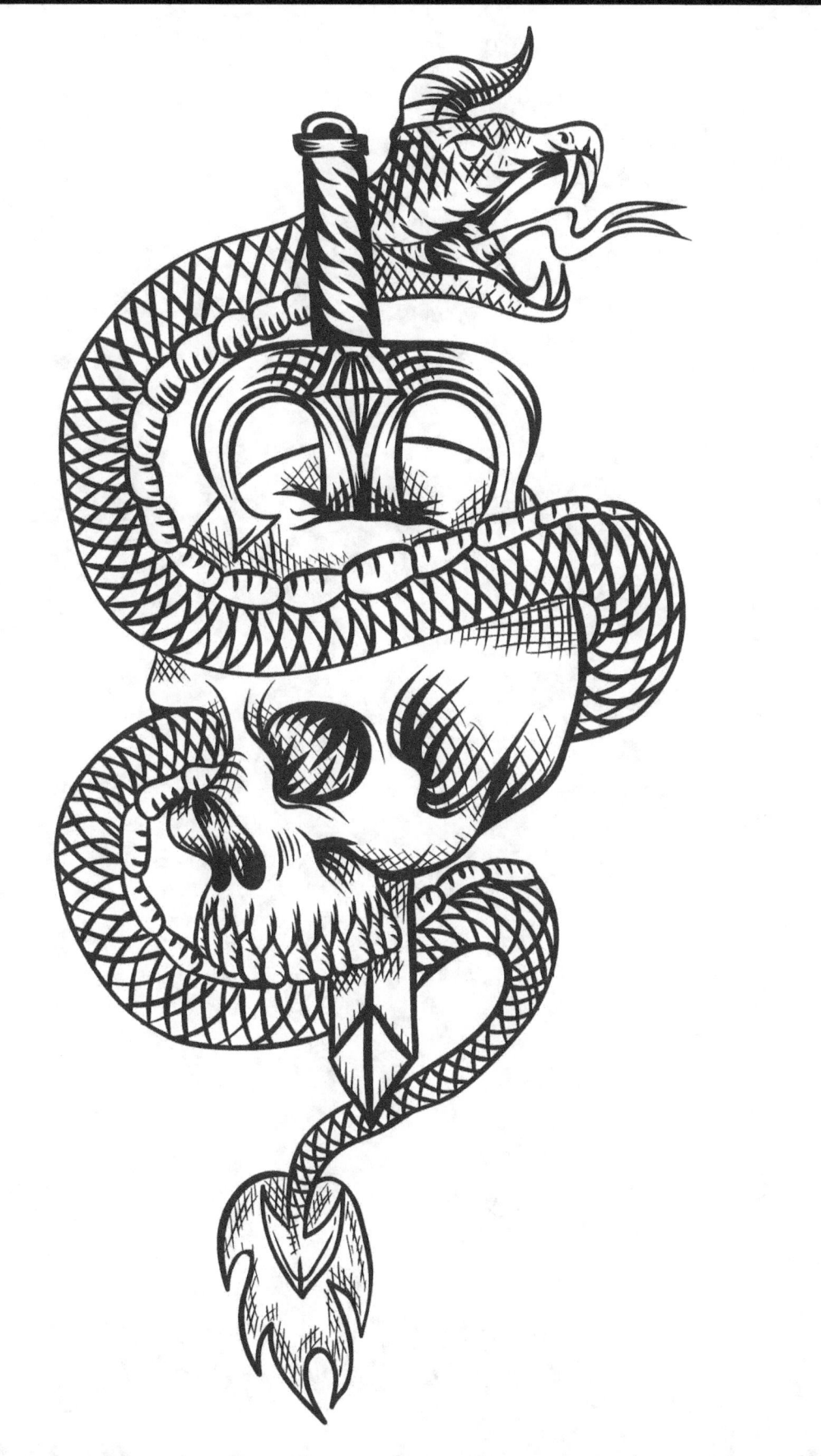

SWORD & SNAKE

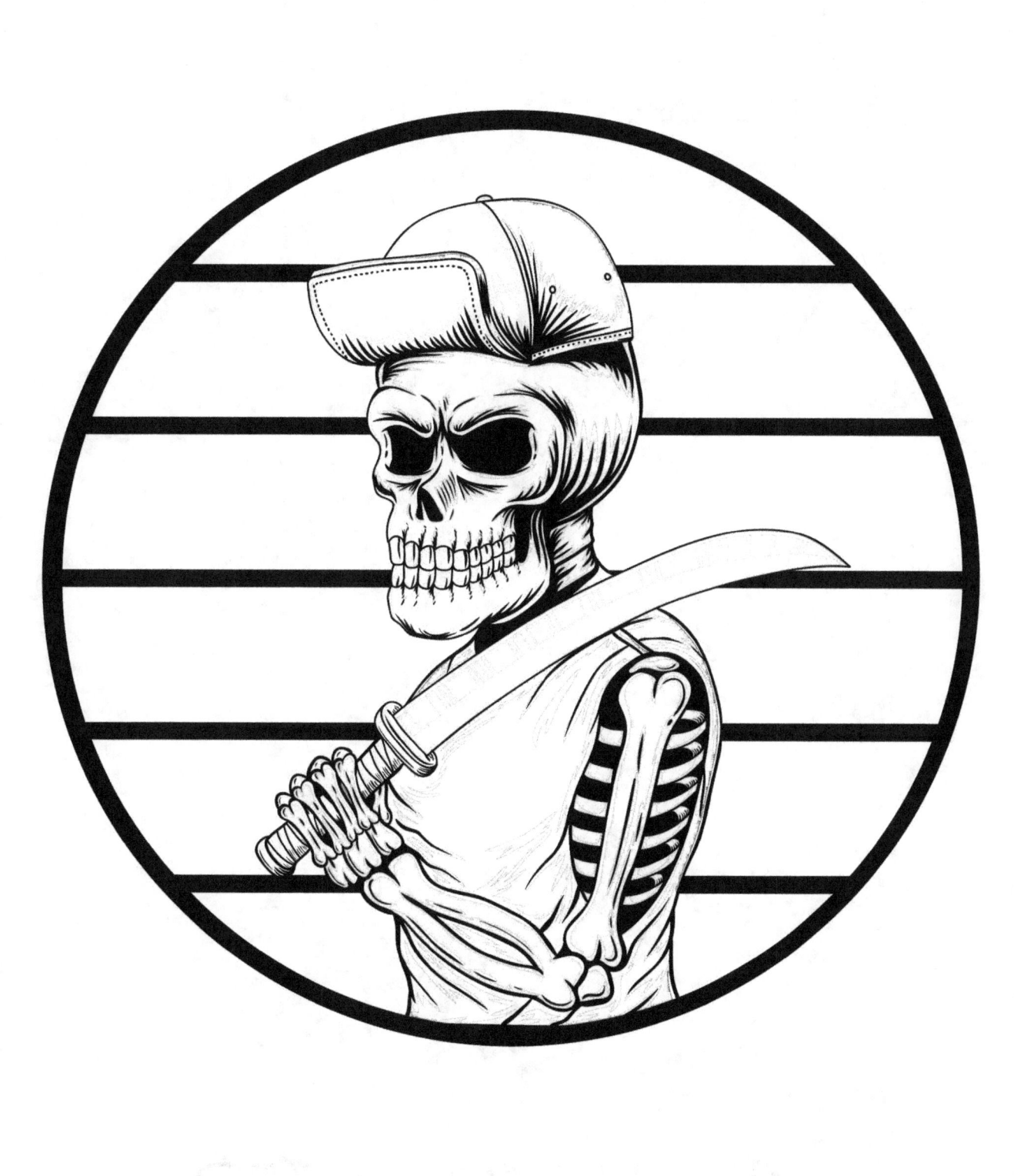

SKULL GANGSTER

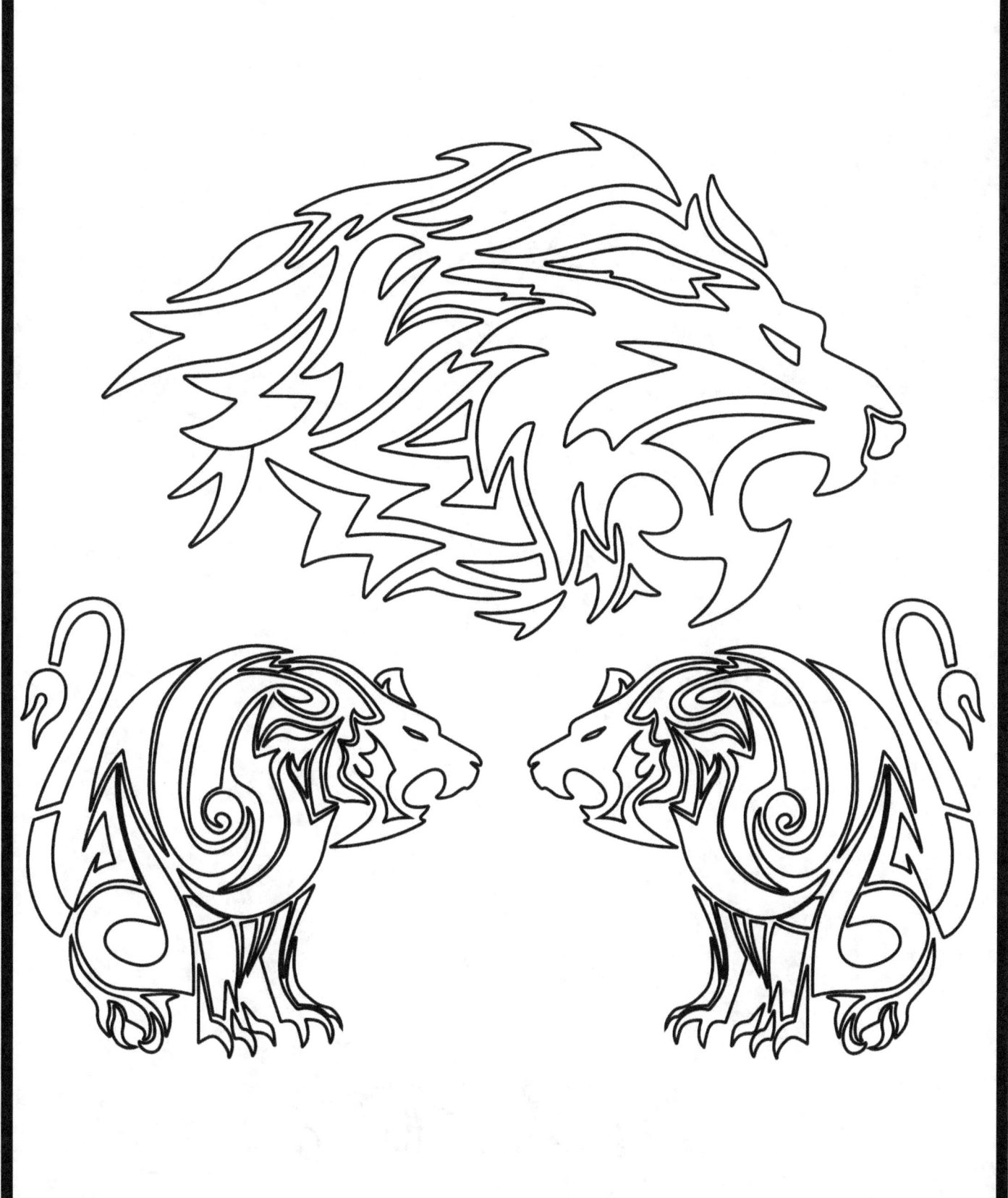

TRIBAL LIONS

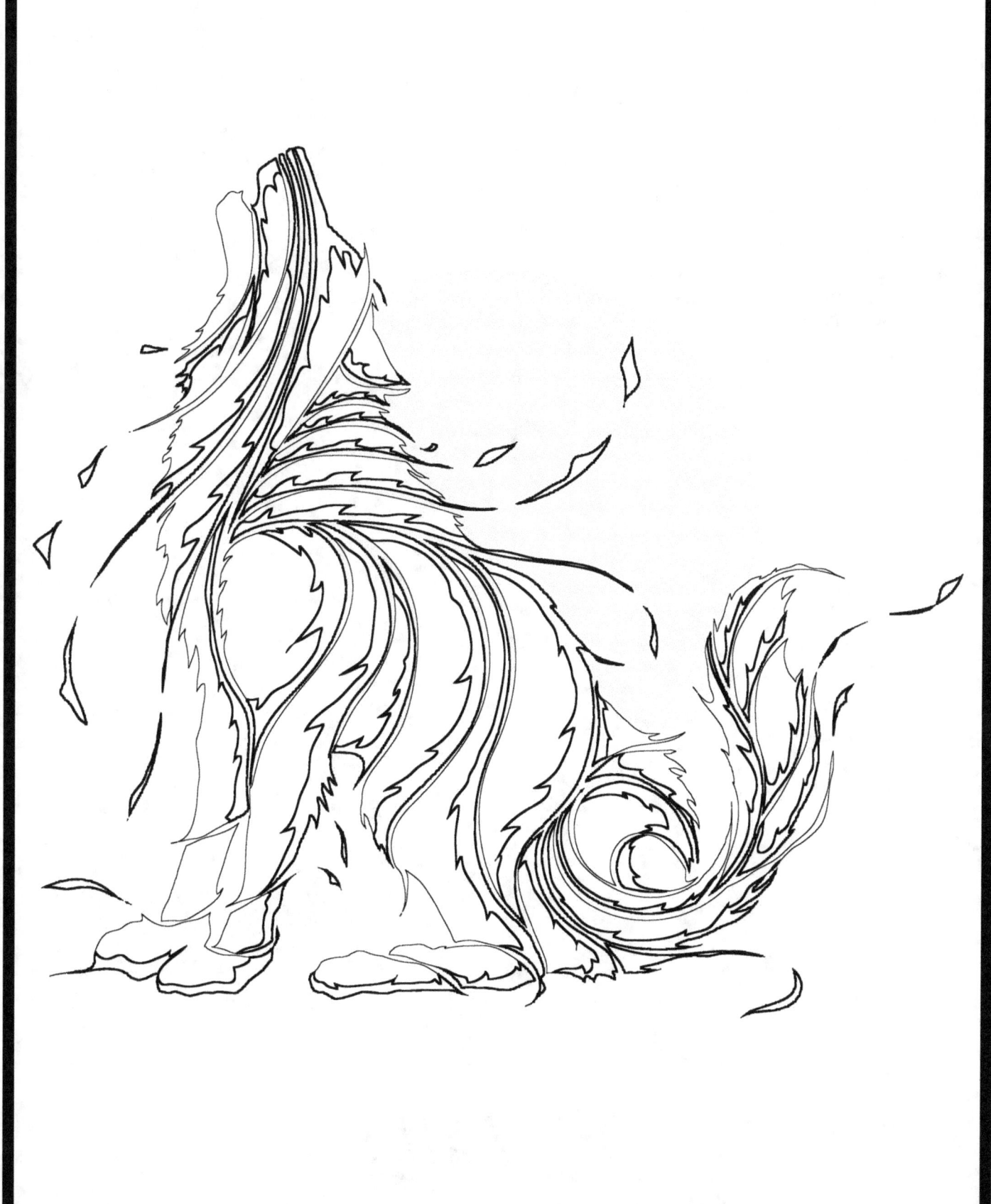

THE WOLF

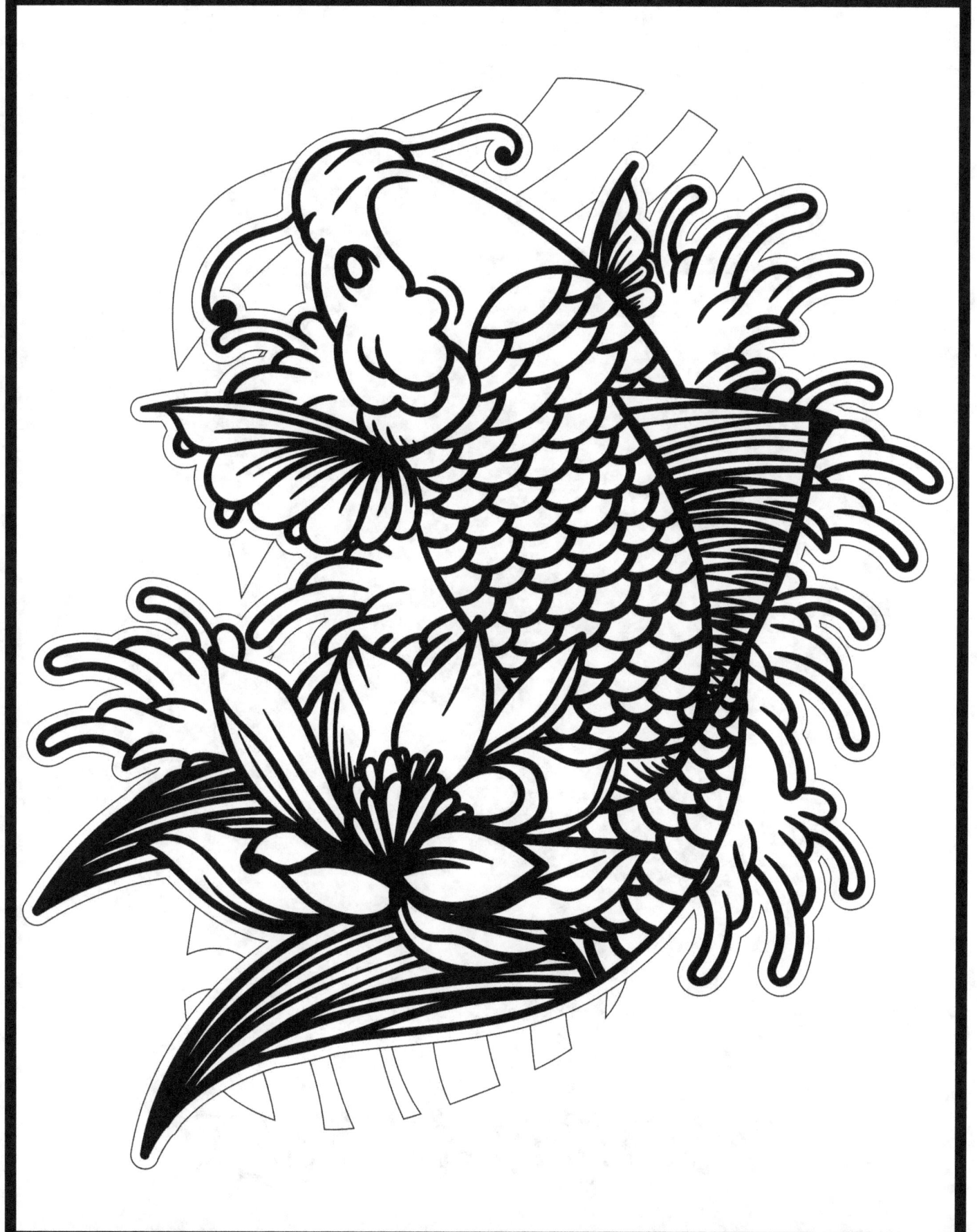

KOI FISH & A FLOWER

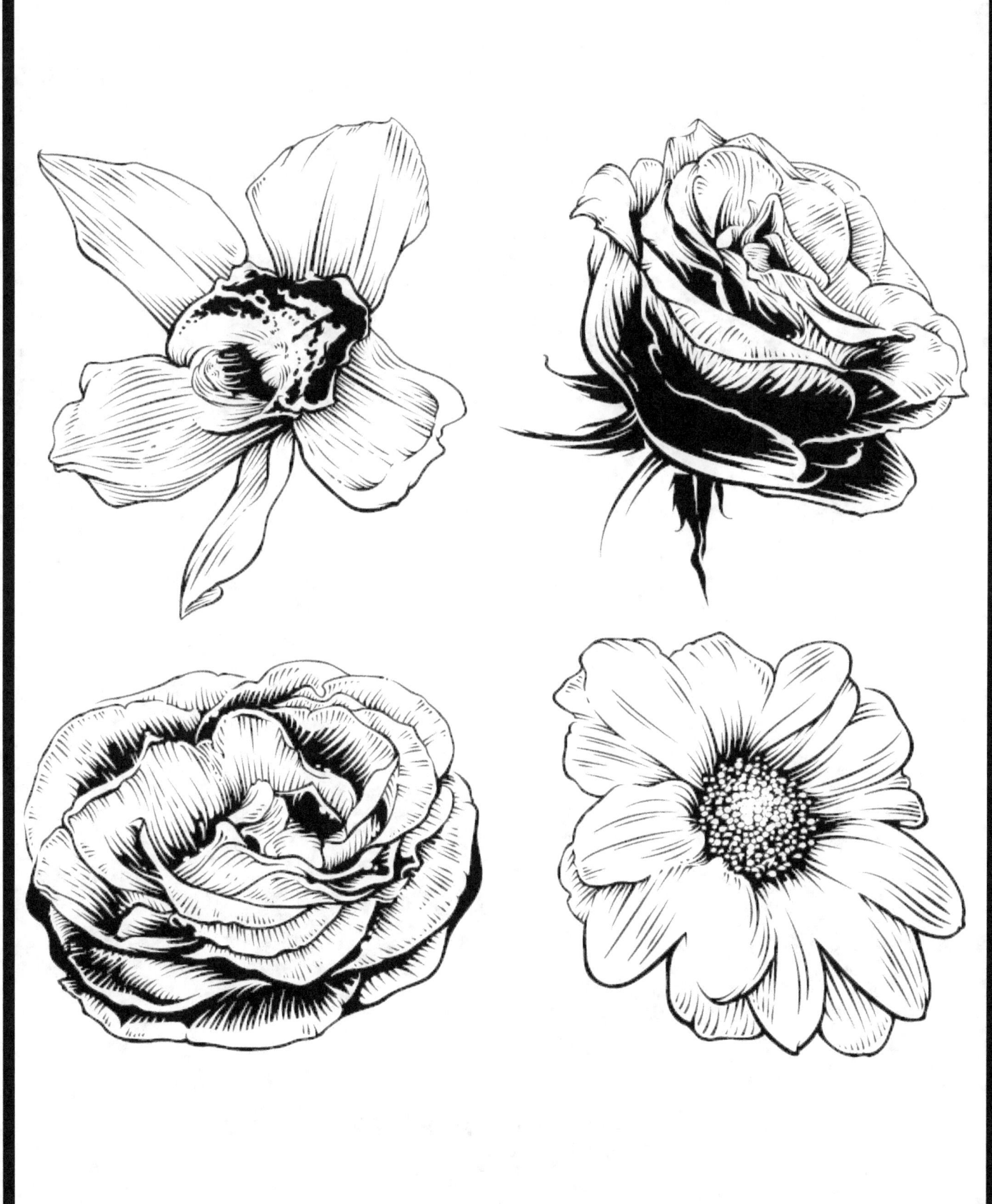

FLOWERS

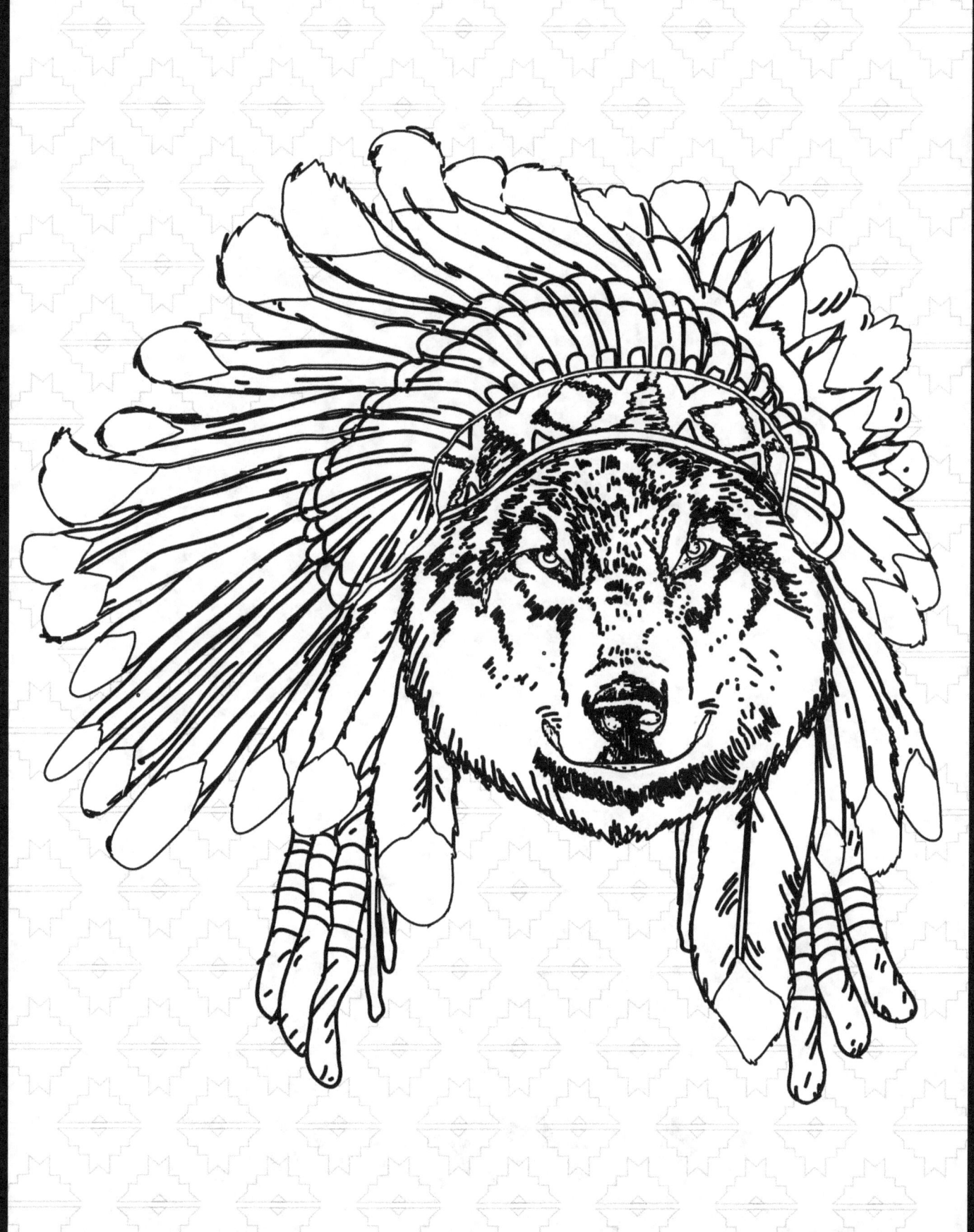

WAR BONNET WOLF

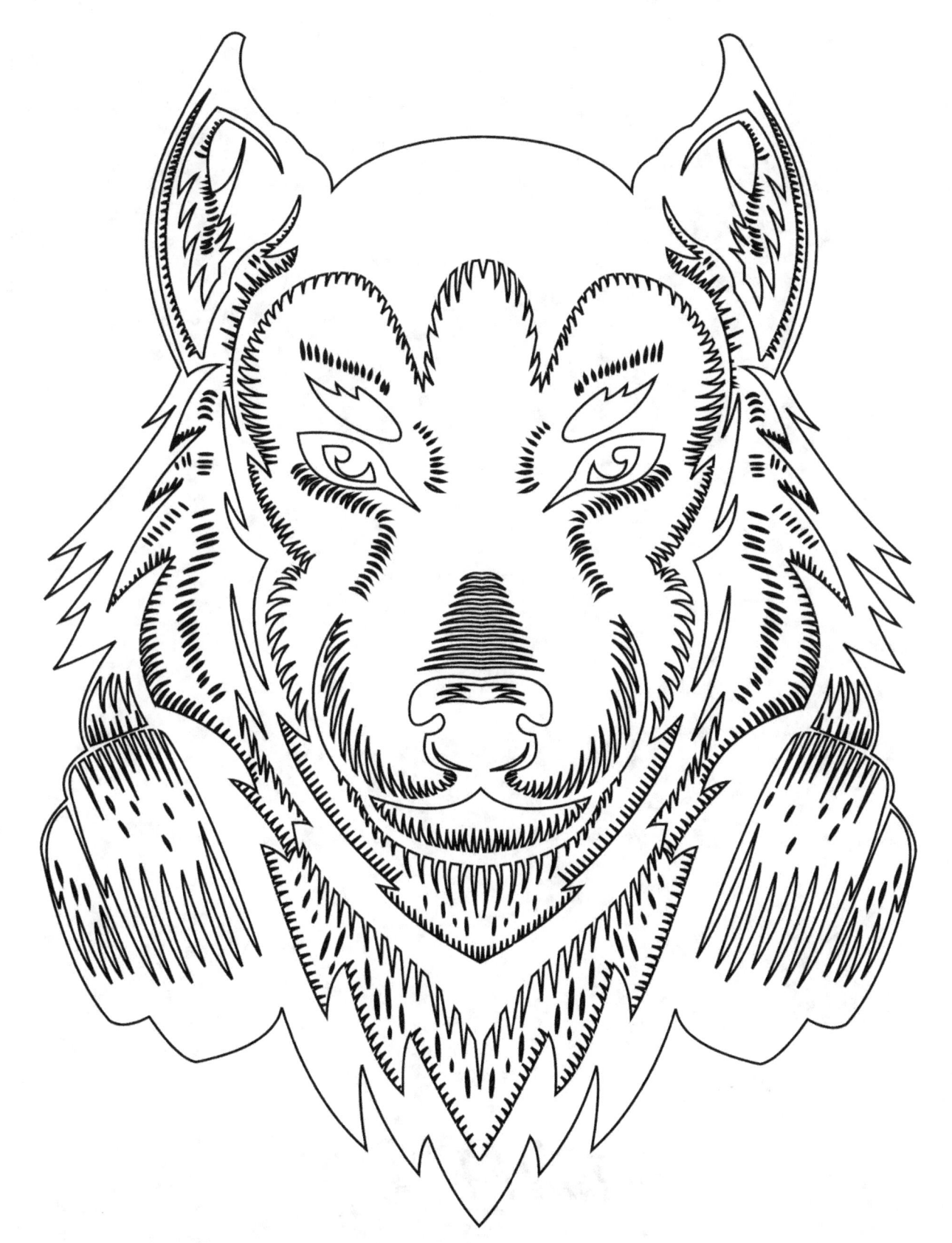

WOLF DJ

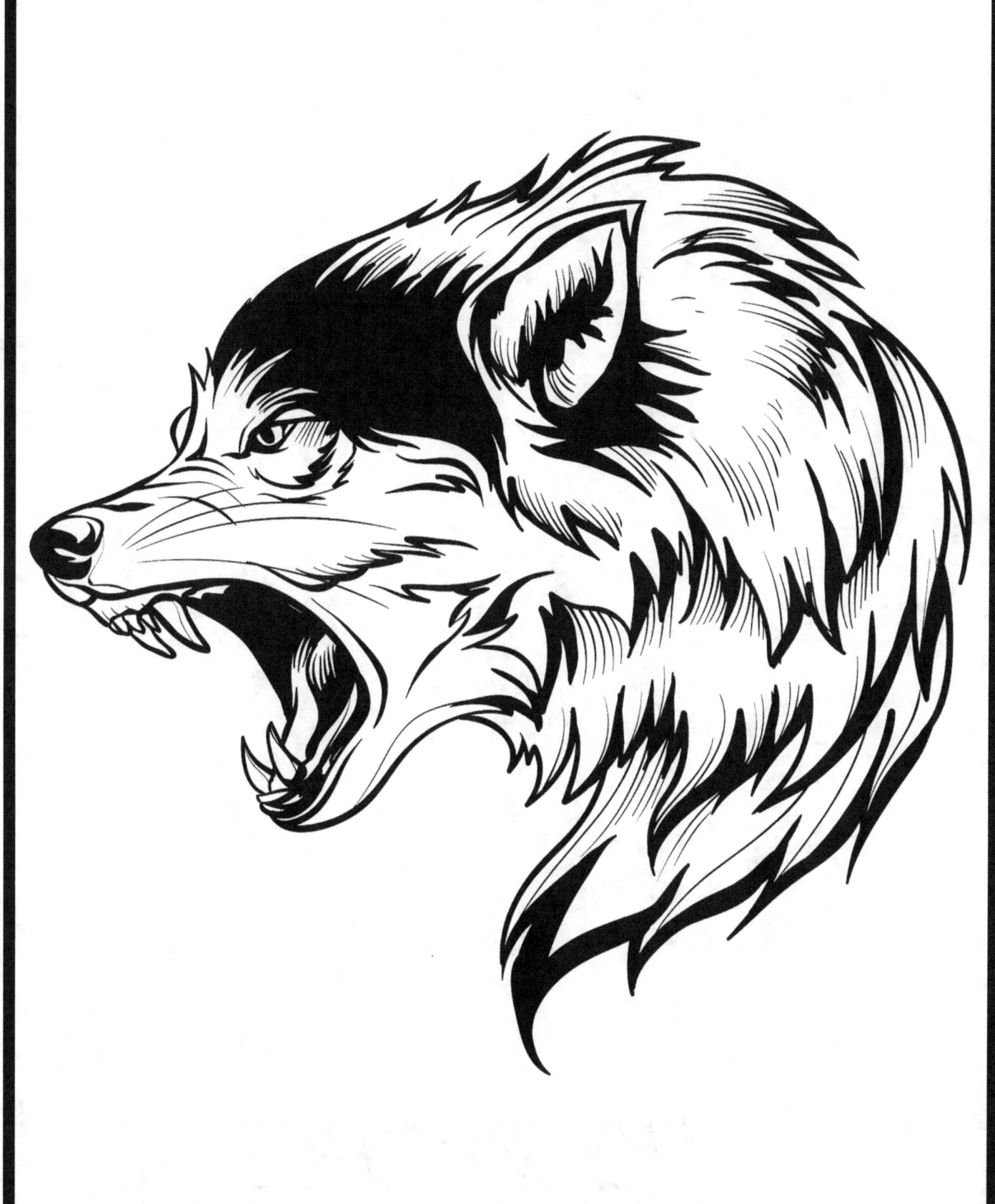

WOLF SIDE FACE

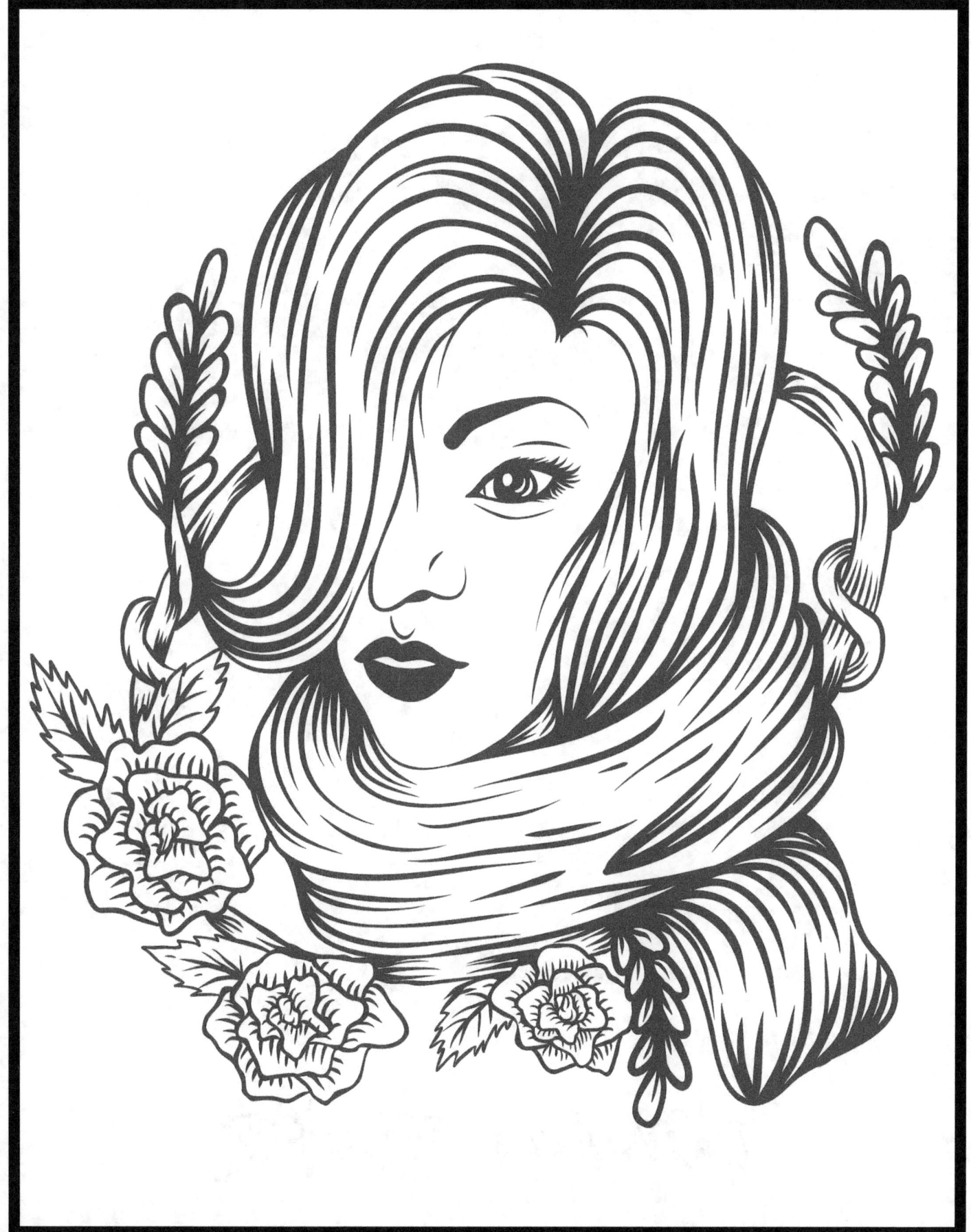

WOMAN & FLOWERS

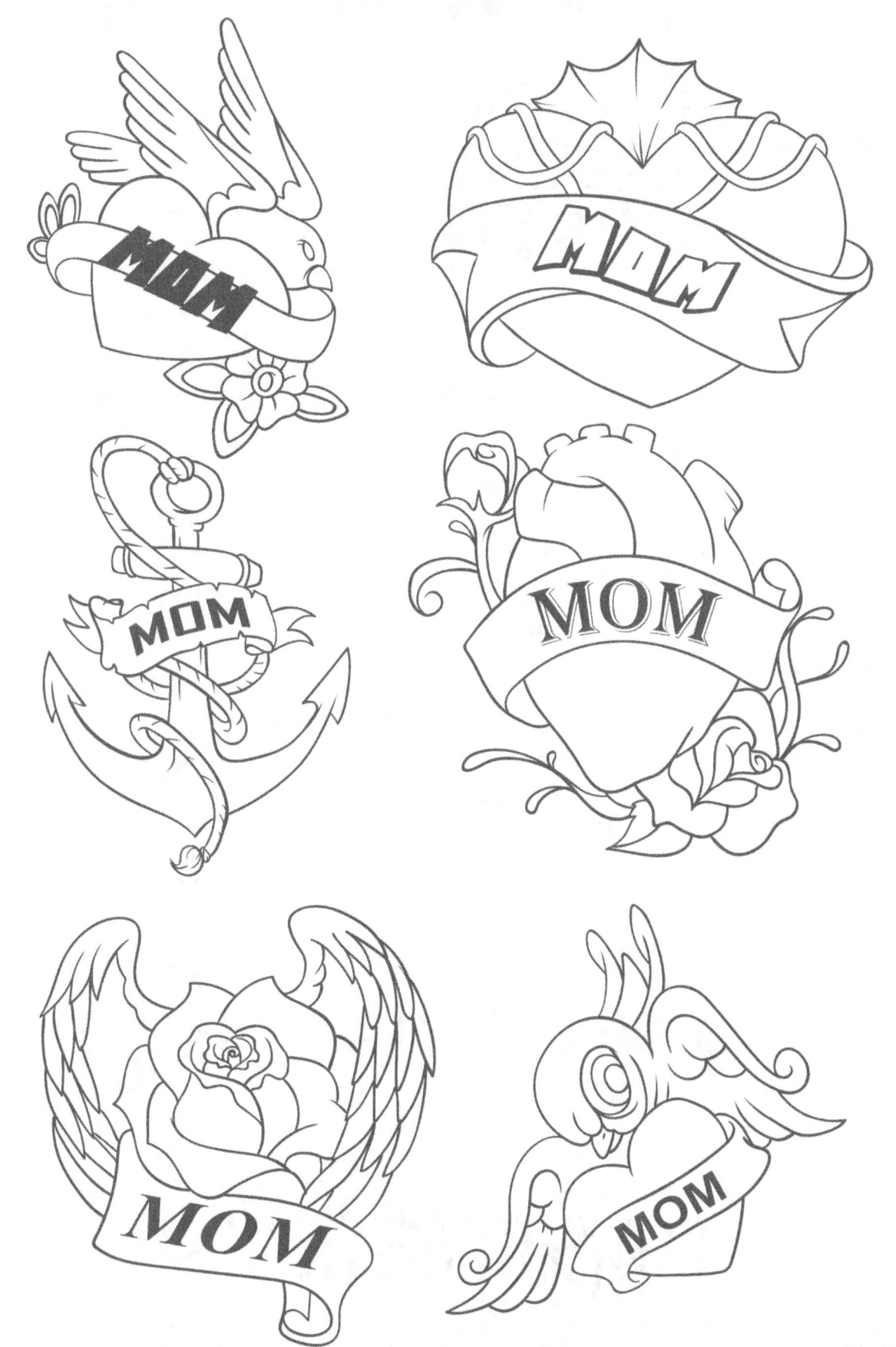

MOM HEARTS

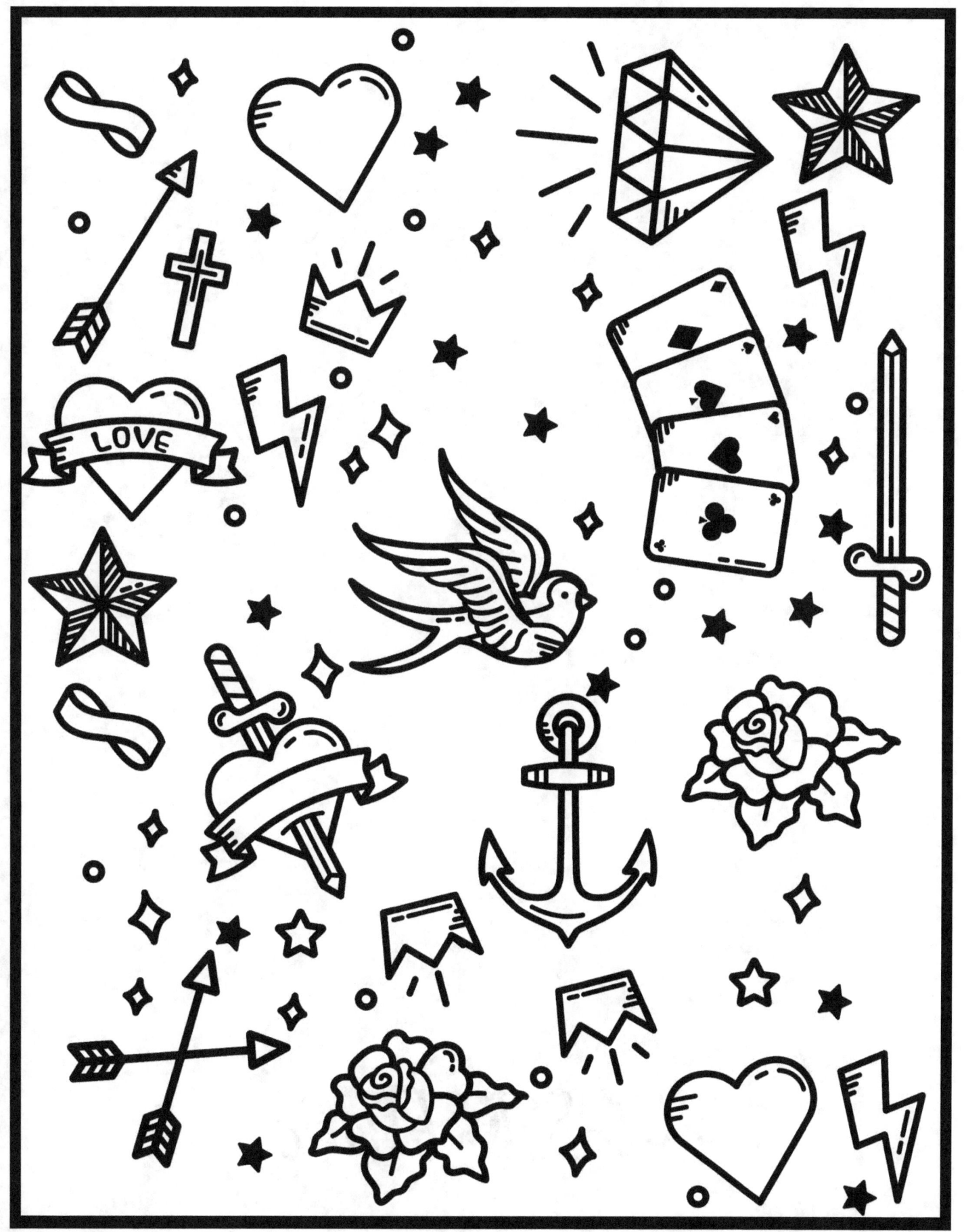

CLASSIC TATTOS

www.ingramcontent.com/pod-product-compliance
Lightning Source LLC
Chambersburg PA
CBHW081501220526
45466CB00008B/2735